THE RIDDLE OF THE *RĀMĀYAṆA*

THE RIDDLE OF THE *RĀMĀYAṆA*

C. V. VAIDYA

GYAN

Published by

Gyan Publishing House
5, Ansari Road
Daryaganj, New Delhi-110002
Phone: 011-47034999, 9811692060
E-mail: books@gyanbooks.com

Distribution Network
gyanbooks.com
India, USA, Canada, UK, Australia

ISBN: 978-93-6780-494-0 (PB)

First Published, 1906

2nd Impression 2024

Printed at: Gyan Press, Delhi.

THE RIDDLE OF THE *RĀMĀYAṆA*
Author: C. V. VAIDYA

THE RIDDLE OF THE *RĀMĀYANA*

by

The late C. V. VAIDYA
M.A., LL. B.

MEHARCHAND LACHHMANDAS
Oriental Publishers & Booksellers
Kucha Chailan, Daryaganj, Delhi 110-006
Sales : **Street No. 1, 1 Ansari Road, Daryaganj, Delhi (India)**

PREFACE

Being encouraged by the favourable manner in which my first book '*The Mahābhārata—a Criticism*' was received by the public, I am now tempted to place before the reader, as stated in the preface to that book, the second instalment of my ideas, *viz.* my views on the Rāmāyaṇa considered from the poetical and historical stand-points. The Rāmāyaṇa, by which I mean the Rāmāyaṇa of Vālmīki, when considered poetically and historically presents so many aspects and incidents which appear almost inexplicable and therefore imaginary that I have ventured to name this book "The Riddle of the Rāmāyaṇa." The solution of these apparently inexplicable aspects and incidents which I have given in the following pages will, I trust, be found at least interesting if not convincing in every case.

I have in this book adopted the Devanagari character for printing the Sanskrit *ślokas* and sentences quoted. Words, however, like Brahmin, which are of usual occurrence are given in English and in their ordinarily accepted spellings. In other respects this book resembles its predecessor almost wholly.

—C. V. VAIDYA

Bombay, 1906.

Transliteration

अ	a	क्	k	द्	d
आ	ā	ख्	kh	ध्	dh
इ	i	ग्	g	न्	n
ई	ī	घ्	gh	प्	p
उ	u	ङ्	ṅ	फ्	ph
ऊ	ū	च्	c	ब्	b
ऋ	ṛ	छ्	ch	भ्	bh
ए	e	ज्	j	म्	m
ऐ	ai	झ्	jh	य्	y
ओ	o	ञ्	ñ	र्	r
औ	au	ट्	ṭ	ल्	l
विसर्ग (:)	ḥ	ठ्	ṭh	व्	v
		ड्	ḍ	श्	ś
		ढ्	ḍh	ष्	ṣ
		ण्	ṇ	स्	s
		त्	t	ह्	h
		थ्	th		
क्ष्	kṣ	त्र्	tr	ज्ञ्	jñ

CONTENTS

THE RĀMĀYANA AS A POEM

I
THE AUTHOR

The *Rāmāyaṇa* purports to be a historical poem written by a contemporary poet, Vālmīki, who is himself an actor in its tragedy. He protects the discarded queen of Rāma, brings up the twin-sons whom she gave birth to, composes a poem on the stirring incidents of their lives and teaches their sons to sing it. The poem is sung by them in the presence of Rāma himself on the occasion of a sacrifice to which Vālmīki has been invited. The tragical and almost heart-rending result of the recitation is well-known. The trembling disheartened loving Sītā comes forward and swears that if she is a really pure mother earth will hide her in her womb. And in ready response to this fearful invocation of the pure queen, her mother comes out from the bosom of the earth seated on a heavenly throne and seizing her darling daughter, disappears. The dismayed Rāma clutches at his wand and is ready to pursue mother earth, but is dissuaded by the assembled sages. The young princes are then acknowledged by Rāma and they console the remainder of his unhappy life.

Such is the story of the composition of the epic as given in the poem itself. Another equally interesting incident bearing on the composition of the poem is related in it in another place. Vālmīki while rambling in the forest in which he lived, saw a hunter kill with an arrow a male crane as he was pairing with his female companion. The sight of the dying crane and his crying consort moved the heart of the kind Ṛṣi who in his excited feelings gave vent to an imprecation which naturally assumed the form of a metrical utterance. That verse well-known in Sanskrit literature may well be quoted here—

मा निषाद प्रतिष्ठां त्वमगमः शाश्वतीः समाः ।
यत्क्रौञ्चमिथुनादेकमवधीः काममोहितम् ॥

The sage was however pleased with the rhythm of his own utterance and must at the same time have forcibly been reminded of the then fresh story of the abduction of Sītā by the Rākṣasa king, Rāvaṇa. He there upon resolved to celebrate the life and exploits of Rāma in a poem composed of verses made on the model of that *śloka*. The first metrical utterance of the primeval poet was greeted by gods and sages and Brahmā himself came down from heaven to congratulate him on the unique position attained by him *viz.* that of the first poet.

The above story curiously enough coincides with the theory maintained in modern days that metrical composition must originally have been prompted by excited feelings. Hazlitt defines poetry to be "the natural impression of any object or event by its vividness exciting an involuntary movement of imagination or passion and producing by sympathy a certain modulation of the voice or sounds expressing it." This circumstance seems to give an air of truth to the story related above. It seems probable that Vālmīki was the first Ṛṣi who adapted the Vedic *chandas* to the composition of poems in classical Sanskrit. For verse loose and simple as it was, when the Vedic hymns were composed, ceased to be attractive to the later Ṛṣis and Ācāryas who composed the Brāhmaṇas and Āraṇyakas in pure and simple prose and the tendency to compose concise *sūtras* or aphorisms had also begun to arise. At such a time Vālmīki revived the Vedic metres in a better and more regulated form and gave a fresh impetus to the writing of poetry. A comparison of the Vedic and classical metres is a subject of great interest, and we may compare some of them here to show how Vālmīki must have improved upon the Vedic metres. The Anuṣṭubh consists of 4 *padas* or lines, each line consisting of eight syllables. No restriction, however, is placed on the respective length or shortness of these syllables. The Anuṣṭubh of classical Sanskrit introduced by Vālmīki brought in two restrictions *viz.* that the 5th syllable of the first and third lines should be long while the 7th of the second and fourth should be short. A sort of rhythm more defined than that of the Vedic metres was thus introduced. A far more stringent system was gradually adopted for longer metres so that the length or shortness of every syllable has now been unalterably fixed and settled. Of course the order of long and short was determined by copying the order of the long and short of some of the most rythmical Vedic *mantras.* To take concrete instances the अनुष्टुभ् *mantra*

सहस्रशीर्षा पुरुषः सहस्राक्षः सहस्रपात् ।
स भूमिं विश्वतो वृत्वाऽत्यतिष्ठद्दशांगुलम् ॥

would very well serve for any Anuṣṭubh *śloka* of classical Sanskrit. The following त्रिष्टुभ् however of the Vedas needs a few changes to be read like इंद्रवज्रा or उपेंद्रवज्रा of the classical literature.

Vedic	*Classical*
उदीर्ष्व नार्यभिजीवलोकम्	उदीर्ष्वं नारी अभिजीवलोकम्
गतासुमेतमुपशेष एहि	गतासुमेतं उपशेष एहि ।
हस्तग्राभस्य दिधिषोस्तवेदं	हस्तग्रभस्या दिधिषोस्तवेदं
पत्युर्जनित्वमभिसंबभूव ।	पत्युर्जनित्वं अभिसंबभूव ॥

We can thus see how easily Vālmīki adapted the Vedic Anuṣṭubh metre to modern Sanskrit. And his example was followed by many poets notably Vyāsa whose work, the *Mahābhārata,* still shows the transitional stage in which the त्रिष्टुभ् and other longer metres were in the process of being transformed into इंद्रवज्रा and उपेंद्रवज्रा metres of modern verse. For Vyāsa's longer *ślokas* often exhibit the unbound license of long and short which obtained in Vedic times. Vālmīki probably wrote in Anuṣṭubh only. The *ślokas* of longer metres which we find in the *Rāmāyaṇa* were all subsequently introduced, as we shall hereafter see, when the *Rāmāyaṇa* was recast.

Vālmīki thus appears to be justly styled the father of modern or classical Sanskrit poetry, as Brahmā is represented to be the father of archaic or Vedic Sanskrit poetry. Both are always referred to in Sanskrit literature as the first poets. See कवेराद्यस्य शासनात् of *Raghu.*, XV.41 and तेने ब्रह्महृदा य आदि कवये of the first *śloka* of *Bhāgavata*. Vālmīki's reputation as the poet par excellence or the *first* classical poet is so well established that he is also simply called *the poet*, कविर्वाल्मीकिशुकयोरिति विश्वः । See also *Raghu.*, XV.32—कविः कुशलवावेव चकार किल नामतः ।

The title of "the first poet" is sometimes explained by Sanskritists as the first writer of *sargabandha kāvya i.e.* a poem divided into *sargas* of which definitions are to be found in standard works on *kāvya* or Poetics. This explanation is opposed to the story related above *viz.* that Vālmīki gave utterance to the first classical verse in the excitement of his feelings. According to that story Vālmīki is not the author of a particular kind of poetry but of classical verse in general, whereas, before him the sages wrote nothing but prose. Mallinātha's commentary on निषादविद्धाण्डजदर्शनोत्थः। श्लोकत्वमापद्यत यस्य शोकः *Raghu.*, XIV.70 is relevant in this connection : चाण्डालं यदामर्त्सयत् तदाप्रभृति-दत्तानि पद्यान्यभवन् । एवं वाक्यान्येवंति श्रूयते ।

The idea that Vālmīki was the author of the first *sargabandha kāvya* may also be proved untenable on another consideration as shown by Prof. Weber. It appears most probable that in the days of Bhavabhūti *i.e.* till about the 7th century A.D. the *Rāmāyaṇa* was not divided into cantos or *sargas* at all, but into chapters or *adhyāyas*. Bhavabhūti quotes from the *Rāmāyaṇa* directly in his *Uttararāmacarita* and mentions the very place from where he makes the quotation. Says Lava—

बालकांडस्यांतिमे अध्यायेऽयं श्लोकः

प्रकृत्यैव प्रिया सीता रामस्यासीन्महात्मनः ।
प्रियभावः स तु तया स्वगुणैरेव वर्धितः ।।

The *śloka is actually found with a variation in the* last *sarga* of Bālakāṇḍa. Thus the quotation is undoubtedly made from the *Rāmāyaṇa*. But it is alleged to be taken from an *adhyāya* and not a *sarga* and this shows that the *Rāmāyaṇa* was not at all a *sargabandha kāvya* in Bhavabhūti's days. The last *ślokas* at the end of each *sarga* in long and awkward metre now found in the *Rāmāyaṇa* were, it appears, introduced even after Bhavabhūti's time in accordance probably with a newly formed theory that the *Rāmāyaṇa* was a typical *sargabandha kāvya*. If then the original *Rāmāyaṇa* of Vālmīki was not a *sargabandha kāvya*, and Vālmīki is the first poet because he was the first to write in classical verse, authors before him using only prose as in the Brāhmaṇas, Vālmīki must be supposed to have preceded Vyāsa and the Dharmaśāstras which are written in Anuṣṭubh metre as a whole.

Whether Vālmīki was a contemporary of Rāma or not, is a question which cannot be satisfactorily solved. If the first canto of the *Rāmāyaṇa* is as old as Vālmīki he knew of Rāma only by hearsay. If on the other hand the part which Vālmīki plays in the incidents of the poem is considered as having originally belonged to it then he must have been his contemporary. Whether contemporary or not, Vālmīki is an old Ṛṣi who is mentioned in the *Taittirīya Prātiśākhya* and in the *Vājasaneyī Saṁhitā*. His name is mentioned as that of a respected Ṛṣi in the *Mahābhārata* itself and his verses are sometimes directly quoted by Vyāsa. He was probably an inhabitant of some place to the northwest of Ayodhyā, as will appear from the greater geographical knowledge displayed of that part in the *Rāmāyaṇa*.

II

THE PRESENT *RĀMĀYAṆA* IS DIFFERENT FROM THE ORIGINAL POEM OF VĀLMĪKI

That the present *Rāmāyaṇa*, even as it is approved and adopted by the searching and all-respected commentator Kaṭaka, is not the *Rāmāyaṇa* originally written by

Vālmīki, not even the most orthodox thinker will be disposed to doubt. Whoever even cursorily reads the poem, cannot but be struck with the inconsistencies, the severances of connections, juxta-positions of new and old ideas which abound so greatly in the present *Rāmāyaṇa*, whether we take the Bengal or the Bombay text of it. And one cannot but come to the conclusion that the *Rāmāyaṇa* of Vālmīki was substantially reconstructed at some subsequent date.

A few glaring instances of contradiction will here be sufficient to convince those who have not gone through the poem. The first canto is an answer to a question by Vālmīki to Nārada as to who was then the best of kings and Nārada gives the palm to Rāma and recounts the whole history of his life. The canto is thus almost a precis of the whole poem. It seems from this as if Vālmīki knew not Rāma nor his great exploits. And yet further on he says to Sītā in the Uttarakāṇḍa that he knew her father-in-law Daśaratha who was his friend and knows her father Janaka, that he knows why and how Rāma has abandoned her. In fact, Vālmīki knows everything and yet asks Nārada who is the best of kings. Either the first or the second is a subsequent interpolation. Again, Sugrīva in the Kiṣkindhā-kāṇḍa first says that he does not know the abode of the evil Rākṣasa (Rāvaṇa) nor his prowess, nor his family.

न जाने निलयं तस्य सर्वथा पापरक्षसः ।
सामर्थ्यं विक्रमं वापि दौष्कुलेयस्य वा कुलम् ॥

And yet further on Sugrīva gives a detailed description of the whole world to the search parties sent by him and therein describes Laṅkā itself mentioning the fact that that country belonged to Rāvaṇa.

स हि देशस्तु वध्यस्य रावणस्य दुरात्मनः ।
राक्षसाधिपतेर्वीराः सहस्राक्षसमद्युतेः ॥

Even Kabandha extols Sugrīva's knowledge of all the places inhabited by Rākṣasas.

स हि स्थानानि कार्त्स्न्येन सर्वाणि कपिकुंजरः ।
नरमांसाशिनां लोके नैपुण्यादधिगच्छति ॥

The inconsistency is irreconcileable. The commentator sees the evident contradiction herein involved and makes a frantic effort at reconciliation by remarking that न जाने means तज्जाने एवंति शेषः। In fact the commentator makes a negative sentence mean exactly the corresponding affirmative. But the difficulty of explaining the next *śloka* which follows न जाने निलयं तस्य &c. is insuperable. For therein Sugrīva says—

सत्यं तु प्रतिजानामि त्यज शोकमरिंदम् ।
करिष्यामि तथा यत्नं यथा प्राप्स्यसि मैथिलीम् ॥

If Sugrīva did not know the abode of Rāvaṇa, his saying "but I swear truly, give up thy wailing; I will make such effort that thou shalt soon recover thy Sītā" is consistent. But if he *knew* his abode as the commentator would have it, he should not have said "but" or तु in the next *śloka*; he should have said "and" or च *i.e.*, "and I know his abode and I swear that thou wilt soon recover thy lost love." It is needless to comment further on the opinion of the commentator. Candidly speaking the geographical description of the whole world given by Sugrīva is, as we shall show hereafter, a subsequent interpolation which formed no part of the original poem of Vālmīki. Forgeries always expose themselves, and the numerous additions, alterations and amplifications in the *Rāmāyaṇa* are so evident that the conclusion cannot be avoided that the text of Vālmīki has been recast almost wholly and by unskilful hands.

The old nucleus of the *Rāmāyaṇa* is, however, easily distinguishable from the vast accretions which have gathered round it. It essentially belongs to that ancient period of Indian History when sacrifice was the most distinguishing feature of Aryan worship, when Buddhism was unknown, when idol-worship did not exist, when Brahmins and Kṣatriyas freely ate animal food, when women learnt the Vedas and performed Vedic rites, when Kṣatriyas competed with Brahmins in learning and Brahmins competed with Kṣatriyas in archery. If we scan the life of Rāma and Sītā, Daśaratha and Kausalyā, Bhāradvāja and Agastya, we find a state of society entirely dissimilar to our own, a society uncontaminated with the feelings and circumstances to which Buddhism has given rise. Rāma fails not to perform a sacrifice himself in consecration of the hut built by Lakṣmaṇa and offers in oblation the flesh of deer specially killed for the occasion. The fact that Lakṣmaṇa roasts a whole deer must strike us, accustomed as we are to vegetable food and even vegetable sacrifices for centuries, as something very startling;

अयं सर्वः समस्तांगः श्रितः कृष्णमृगो मया ।
देवता देवसंकाश यजस्व कुशलो ह्यसि ॥

When Rāma performs the last obsequies of Jaṭāyu, he offers venison to the departed bird;

रोहिमांसानि चोत्कृत्य पेशीकृत्वा महायशाः ।
शकुनाय ददौ रामः रम्ये हरितशाद्वले ॥

Again, he is an adept in reciting the Vedic *mantras* on the various occasions in man's life—

राघवोपि महातेजा नावमारुह्य तां ततः ।
ब्रह्मवत्क्षत्रवच्चैव जजाप हितमात्मनः ॥

And further on—

यत्तत्प्रेतस्य मर्त्यस्य कथयंति द्विजातयः ।
तत्स्वर्गगमनं क्षिप्रं तस्य रामो जजाप ह ॥

The poet nowhere fails to describe how Rāma performed his *sandhyā* every day. In fact Rāma's proficiency in Vedic *mantras* and his strict observance of Vedic rites could not be less than those of any rigid Brahmin. In Rāma's time even women performed sacrifices and made their *sandhyā* obeisance. When Rāma went to see Kausalyā after the order for his banishment had been obtained by Kaikeyī from her husband, she was performing a sacrifice not in the presence of her husband but by herself with Vedic *mantras* —

सा क्षौमवसना हृष्टा नित्यं व्रतपरायणा ।
अग्निं जुहोति स्म तदा मंत्रवत् कृतमंगला ॥

When Māruti did not find Sītā after his wearisome search for her, he sat on a tree by the side of a beautiful rivulet in the Aśokavana of Rāvaṇa, believing that she would come to that very stream early in the morning to perform her *sandhyā*.

संध्याकालमना: श्यामा ध्रुवमेष्यति जानकी ।
नदीं चेमां शुभजलां संध्यार्थे वरवर्णिनी ॥

A woman performing *sandhyā*—woman who is now believed to be incapable of learning the Vedas—seems passing strange to our ears. And it did so strike the ears of the modern commentator also, for he remarks—

किंच सम्यग्भगवद्ध्यानस्यैव संध्यापदार्थत्वेनास्त्येव तत्र स्त्रिया अधिकार: ।
गायत्रीमंत्रेण तदर्थस्मरणपूर्वकध्याने तु द्विजस्यैवाधिकार इत्यन्यत् ।

[Sandhyā simply means contemplation of God and hence in that sense a woman has permission to perform *sandhyā*. It is entirely another thing that only a *dvija* or a twice born has the right to perform *sandhyā* in the sense of contemplation of God by knowing and reciting the Gāyatrī *mantra]*. This is however an unwarranted quibble; for what worship women are now allowed to perform, cannot be and is not styled संध्या. And what should we think when we are told that Kausalyā killed by her own hands the sacrificial horse with three sword strokes.

कौसल्या तं हयं तत्र परिचर्य समंतत: ।
कृपाणैर्विशशासैनं त्रिभि: परमया मुदा ॥

She must have been a very strong and a true Rajput lady indeed.

The pictures of the Āśramas of Bhāradvāja and Agastya are very interesting. Fond of retired scenes of great natural beauty and intensely religious and monastic in their occupation and spirit, the Ṛṣis passed their time in ablutions, in study, in contemplation and in sacrificing. Yet they were not strangers to what was passing around them and raised their own subsistence from fields ploughed with their own hands. When compelled by necessity, they took up arms in defence of themselves, their sacrifices and their cultivations. Then again they ate flesh like their Kṣatriya friends.

पंच पंचनखा भक्ष्या ब्रह्मक्षत्रेण राघव ।

They could sacrifice a cow in मधुपर्क.

उपानयत धर्मात्मा गामर्घ्यमुदकं ततः ।

There was no idol-worship in their devotion; their huts contained separate sacrificial alters for the various deities of the Vedas—Indra, Varuṇa, Yama and so on.[1] These and other similar circumstances disclose a state of society which existed long before the rise of Buddhism, a society accustomed to the adoration of Vedic deities by sacrifice, a society in which the Brahmins and Kṣatriyas were not separated by an unbridgeable gulf, a society in which women played as strong and independent a part as men. Undoubtedly such was the time of Vālmīki, the author of the *Rāmāyaṇa*. It is impossible that any poet who lived about the beginning of the Christian era (when the *Rāmāyaṇa*, as we shall soon show, assumed its present shape) should have such ideas in his mind though such ideas existing in a poem already respected might be retained from a feeling of sanctity attached to them.

1. Rāma's place also contained a separate Āyatana for Viṣṇu. श्रीमत्यायतने विष्णोः शिश्ये नरवरात्मजः ॥ II. 6, 4. The commentator wrongly explains this by saying निजभवनवर्ति देवपूजालये. If it were a देवपूजालय why is it called Viṣṇu's house? It appears that Rāma's palace had separate sacrificial apartments for each of the Vedic gods in the same way as the humble habitation of Agastya.

III

THE DATE OF THE COMPILATION OF THE *RĀMĀYAṆA* IN ITS PRESENT FORM

The foregoing considerations will easily enable us to distinguish the old nucleus of the *Rāmāyaṇa* from the overgrown accretions by its substance and sometimes by its form. Whenever we find new ideas or whenever we find *ślokas* with long metres and complex *alaṅkāras*, we may be sure that they have been subsequently added. It is unquestioned that such additions are being made down to the present day; for we find in our present edition long cantos which have been declared by Kaṭaka himself as प्रक्षिप्त or interpolated, and cantos which were not in existence even in his time. We have already adverted to the fact that the *Rāmāyaṇa* was not divided into cantos at all, but into chapters so late as in the days of Bhavabhūti. It, however, seems probable that the *Rāmāyaṇa* of Vālmīki was substantially reconstructed or recast at one particular time, though minor additions or alterations may have been made subsequently at different times. It will therefore be useful to inquire when this last edition of the *Rāmāyaṇa* was compiled.

We can fix the limits within which the present edition of the *Rāmāyaṇa* must have been compiled with tolerable accuracy. Whoever reads the *Rāmāyaṇa* of Vālmīki and the *Raghuvaṁśa* of Kālidāsa side by side, will be convinced that Kālidāsa must have had before him the *Rāmāyaṇa* of Vālmīki as it essentially is at the present day; for he follows very closely the details of the story as they are related in the *Rāmāyaṇa* of to-day. Nay, sometimes he uses the very words of the *Rāmāyaṇa e.g.* श्लोकत्वमापद्यत यस्य शोकः, अरावणमरामं वा, etc.

It is, therefore, certain that the present form of the *Rāmāyaṇa* precedes the *poet celebre*. The date of Kālidāsa has been differently fixed. Some place him in the beginning of the Christian era; others on more carefully sifted basis, place him in the fifth century A.D. Even taking the latter date, there is another reason which should induce us to place the present form of the *Rāmāyaṇa* long anterior to him. The stories related in the present edition of the *Rāmāyaṇa*, marvellous as they are, were not sufficient to satisfy the popular craving for marvels and wonders. Nay as we shall see subsequently the story of Rāma's life has been constantly changing since its first inauguration by the gradual increase of the marvellous element in it. The various versions that exist to-day can, by this very consideration, *viz.*, the extent of the marvellous element in them, be arranged in chronological order. We will develop this subject more extensively when we consider the different versions which intervened between the original *Rāmāyaṇa* of Vālmīki and its amplification into its present form. Here we refer to the subject so far as the marvellous element has gradually increased *since* that amplification.

Innumerable as the modern versions are, they may be arranged under three distinct heads—(i) the version of the poets beginning with Kālidāsa; (ii) the version of the Purāṇas typified by that of the *Padma-purāṇa* or the *Adhyātma Rāmāyaṇa*; (iii) the version of the vernacular poets of which that of Tulasīdāsa may be taken as the type. When one minutely considers how the story of the *Rāmāyaṇa* even as it is, has been gradually changed, so far as the marvellous element is concerned, nay, when one compares what one actually finds in the present *Rāmāyaṇa* with what orthodox Hindus ordinarily believe without carefully looking into the *Rāmāyaṇa* itself, one is really amazed to find what an amount of unfounded exaggeration has crept into popular belief and has distorted an originally tolerably believable story. It would be tedious to collect here all such exaggerations and we will content ourselves with giving the most glaring instances of them so that one may be able to judge what a long time must have elapsed between the *Rāmāyaṇa* of Vālmīki in its present form and Kālidāsa's *Raghuvaṁśa*.

I. According to the present *Rāmāyaṇa*, Rāma appears to have had many wives. Kālidāsa and later poets mention that he had one wife only.[1] The present *Rāmāyaṇa* seems to represent that Rāma had one महिषी or crowned queen but had many other wives (not concubines) as was usual with Kṣatriya princes in his days. Says Mantharā to Kaikeyī in the *Rāmāyaṇa*.

हृष्टाः खलु भविष्यन्ति रामस्य परमाः स्त्रियः ।
अप्रहृष्टा भविष्यन्ति स्नुषास्ते भरतक्षये ॥

The commentator says nothing on this *śloka;* in fact it is impossible to suggest that स्त्रियः simply means the handmaids and attendants of Sītā for that word is evidently in contrast with स्नुषाः or daughters-in-law. And this *śloka* also goes to show that Bharata too had many wives. Daśaratha also is said in the present *Rāmāyaṇa* to have had 350 wives besides his three queens. When he called his wives together as Rāma was about to depart for Daṇḍakāraṇya, "Three hundred fifty young women with red eyes surrounding Kausalyā slowly moved in the observance of a vow."

अर्धसप्तशतास्तत्र प्रमदास्ताम्रलोचनाः ।
कौसल्यां परिवार्याथ शनैर्जग्मुर्धृतव्रताः ॥

No doubt is left about their status as further on they are styled as the mothers of Rāma. Thus it appears that Daśaratha and Bharata and Rāma all had many wives besides their consecrated queens And in this way only can we explain so far as the present *Rāmāyaṇa* is concerned, the fact that when Sītā was banished by Rāma he had her golden image for his wife at the time of the performance of a sacrifice. For, a consecrated queen alone can participate in the performance of a religious ceremony. In the sacrifice of Daśaratha, only his three queens and notably Kausalyā took part in the actual performance of the ceremony. However we may interpret this fact of the golden image of Sītā we cannot get over the *śloka* quoted in the beginning of this paragraph; the import of which is

[1] अनन्यजानेः सैवासीद्यस्माज्जाया हिरण्मयी । —रघुवंश.

plain and unquestionable and we have the strange fact before us *viz.*, that Rāma is represented in the present *Rāmāyaṇa* to have had more wives than one.[1]

II. Equally astonishing is the fact that the present *Rāmāyaṇa* does not represent Ahalyā as transformed into a stone nor did Rāma release her from her metamorphosis by the touch of the dust of his feet. How simple, natural and believable is the story of the *Rāmāyaṇa!* Enraged Gautama cursed his wife thus : "you will remain in this Āśrama unseen by any person, full of repentance, lying in ashes, without food, subsisting only on the air."

वातभक्षा निराहारा तप्यन्ती भस्मशायिनी ।
अदृश्या सर्वभूतानामाश्रमेऽस्मिन्वसिष्यसि ॥

It is not possible to argue that her lying in ashes indicates her being changed into a stone; for, the words वातभक्षा (subsisting on the air), तप्यंती (full of repentance), निराहारा (without food) are important and explicit.[2] Nor does Rāma touch her with his foot; on the contrary he falls at her feet when she voluntarily appears in his presence. "Having finished her penance she came into their sight and the Rāghava princes with gladness fell at her feet."

शापस्यान्तमुपागम्य तेषां दर्शनमागता ।
राघवौ तु तदा तस्याः पादौ जगृहतुर्मुदा ॥

Most probably she had finished her penance, as prescribed by her husband, by the time that Rāma came to the hermitage, and resumed her duty of welcoming to her house a distinguished guest who was thus the occasion of the reconciliation of that unhappily separated pair. Yet Kālidāsa believed and generations since his time have believed

1. Probably this *śloka* has been put in by the last compiler under influence of the manners of his days. The original *Rāmāyaṇa* of Vālmīki probably showed Rāma to have had one wife only.

2. Mark the commentary पुराणादिप्रसिद्धः शिलारूपप्राप्तिशापः कल्पांतरिणः इति न विरोधः । अत्र शिलारूपत्वे तात्पर्यकथने वातभक्षेत्यस्य विरोधः स्पष्ट एवेति केचित् ।

that Ahalyā was transformed into a stone and was freed from that condition by the purifying touch of the dust of Rāma's feet.

प्रत्यपद्यत चिराय यत्पुनः ।
चारु गौतमवधूः शिलामयी ॥
स्वं वपुः स किल किल्बिषच्छिदाम् ।
रामपादरजसामनुग्रहः ॥ *Raghu.*, XI.34

III. The *Rāmāyana* does not represent that a bridge of floating stones was built across the sea between Rameshwaram and Ceylon. It simply says that the monkeys built a cause-way by filling up the sea with huge masses of stones. The popular belief, however, is that the stones floated over the water—a physical impossibility—and Kālidāsa seems to have believed the latter theory. The reference in the *Raghuvaṁśa* is rather ambiguous though his wording leans towards the popular belief—

स सेतुं बंधयामास प्लवगैर्लवणांभसि ।

IV. Whereas even the present edition of the *Rāmāyaṇa* lays no claim to Vālmīki's having foretold the whole of it, Kālidāsa appears to have believed that it had been foretold by inspiration. Probably in Kālidāsa's time and undoubtedly ever since, Vālmīki's *Rāmāyaṇa* was and has come to be so revered as to be looked upon as a revealed work like the Vedas and yet strangely enough it is least read and studied; for otherwise such absurd ideas which are contradicted by what the *Rāmāyaṇa* itself contains would not have gained popular credence. Kālidāsa in his *Raghuvaṁśa* says :

अथ प्राचेतसोपज्ञं रामायणमितस्ततः ।
मैथिलेयौ कुशलवौ जगतुर्गुरुचोदितौ ॥ XV.63

Mallinātha explains प्राचेतसोपज्ञ[1] as प्राचेतसेन आदौ ज्ञातम् (first known by Prācetasa), उपज्ञा ज्ञानमाद्यं स्यादित्यमरः ।

1. A different interpretation might be put upon this word but even then the idea of Vālmīki's *Rāmāyaṇa* being an inspired work still remains.

Now the *Rāmāyaṇa* itself says in the first chapter that Vālmīki asked Nārada who was the best king and that Nārada there upon related Rāma's life. This shows that the *Rāmāyaṇa* was written by Vālmīki after this. If the Uttarakāṇḍa or the very second canto of the first Kāṇḍa is to be believed, the *Rāmāyaṇa* was composed by Vālmīki when Sītā's sons were being reared up in his Aśrama. Even Brahmā's boon to Vālmīki simply says that Vālmīki might know by inspiration what Rāma did in private *i.e.* what Rāma did not do in public. In either case it is certain that the *Rāmāyaṇa* was not a revealed or inspired work as Kālīdāsa probably thought it to be.

V. भुजमूर्धोरुबाहुल्यादेकोपि धनदानुजः ।
ददृशे स यथापूर्वं मातृवंश इव स्थितः ॥ *Raghu.*, XII.88

shows that Kālīdāsa believed that Rāvaṇa had more than two thighs a thing which, we believe, is nowhere mentioned in the *Rāmāyaṇa* of to-day.[1]

It would be too long to detail here all the new stories which have gained popular credence *since* the days of Kālidāsa. But it would not be out of place or uninteresting to briefly notice a few of them. Sītā's *swayaṁvara* in popular belief is a grand affair wherein many kings participated including Rāvaṇa who having succeeded in raising the bow to his breast fell down with the heavy load on his chest and was only saved by Rāma's raising it up. Nothing of the kind is to be found in the present edition of the *Rāmāyaṇa* or in Kālidāsa. On the contrary, when Rāma lifted up and strung the bow there was no *swayaṁvara* at all and he was all alone. Again, Mantharā is believed to have been an emissary sent by the gods to procure Rāma's banishment to Daṇḍakāraṇya in order that he might destroy Rāvaṇa. This is not to be found in the *Rāmāyaṇa*. The touching scene of Sulocanā, wife of Indrajit, being apprised of the death of her husband by the sudden falling of his arm in her presence, her wailing, and her burning herself as *Satī* has no basis in the orthodox text of the *Rāmāyaṇa*; so also Ahi Rāvaṇa and Mahi Rāvaṇa and the latter's wife Candrāvatī who is promised by Rāma that he would marry her in the next *Avatāra* as Satyabhāmā. Kuśa and Lava in popular story (perhaps since the days of Bhavabhūti or even he might have

It will appear from the foregoing that the present form of the *Rāmāyaṇa* which is almost innocent of marvels, if compared with what people now believe or believed in the days of Kālidāsa, must have been in existence long before him in order that such absurd stories should have gained credence in the teeth of what is stated in the *Rāmāyaṇa* itself. If we take the later date of Kālidāsa, the present *Rāmāyaṇa* must at least have preceded it by three or four centuries and its lowest date cannot, therefore, be later than the second century A.D.

The higher limit for the present compilation of the *Rāmāyaṇa* is supplied to us by other considerations. That compilation unquestionably is later than the rise of Buddhism. There are references to श्रमणs and श्रमणीs in the present edition of the *Rāmāyaṇa*.

तापसा भुंजते चापि श्रमणाश्चैव भुंजते । I, 14,12.

See also या चीरमासाद्य वनस्य मध्ये ।
जाता विसंजा श्रमणीव काचित् ।। II.

The commentator says—श्रमणा बौद्धसंन्यासिनः । यद्वा श्रमणपदः संन्यास्युपलक्षणम्. It may be said that the word *śramaṇa* existed before the rise of Buddhism and its use is, therefore, not sufficient evidence to prove that the present *Rāmāyaṇa* is later than the rise of Buddhism. But there is a direct reference to Buddha himself in the *Rāmāyaṇa* and it contains a downright condemnation of him.

यथा हि चोरः स तथा हि बुद्धः ।
तथागतं नास्तिकमत्र विद्धि ।।
तस्माद्धियः शक्यतमः प्रजानाम् ।
स नास्तिके नाभिमुखो बुधः स्यात् ।।

only incorporated a then existing belief) are not recognized in the tame and humble position of singing boys. They seize the sacrificial horse of Rāma and defeat his generals including Candraketu and even Lakṣmaṇa. Lastly, popular tradition converted the *Rāmāyaṇa* from a tragedy into a comedy inasmuch as Sītā is again accepted by Rāma after some ordeal as his wife. This is perhaps solely the invention of Bhavabhūti who has made use of this part of the story for purposes of his drama, the *Uttararāmacarita*.

Now Buddha must have been reviled when there was a reaction against Buddhism, after Aśoka had established it as a state religion, under the orthodox kings Puṣpamitra and Agnimitra *i.e.*, about 150 B.C. or in the very beginning when he was preaching successfully his doctrines in the 6th century B.C. The first alternative seems more probable and the *Rāmāyaṇa* in its present form cannot be put earlier than the first century B.C.

Another consideration tends towards the same conclusion. The mention of *rāśis* or zodiacal signs in the modern compilation of the *Rāmāyaṇa* proves it to be not earlier than the first century B.C. Up to that time, the Aryans of India regulated their sacrifices by the conjunction of the moon with the several fixed stars. In fact, the astronomy and the astrology of the ancient Aryans were based till then solely on the division of the ecliptic into the 27 constellations. They had no knowledge of the signs of the Zodiac or what are now known as the लग्न्s or *rāśis*, which were evidently introduced by or borrowed from the Greeks, about 200 B.C., for even the Buddhistic scriptures of the days of Aśoka regulate their time by reference to the *nakṣatras* only. Rāma's auspicious birth is thus described in the *Rāmāyaṇa* :—

नक्षत्रे दिविदैवत्ये स्वोच्चसंस्थेषु पंचसु ।
ग्रहेषु कर्कटे लग्ने वाक्पताविंदुना सह ॥ [1]

Thirdly, in the Uttarakāṇḍa the grammatical attainments of Māruti are very highly spoken of. They are also touched in the Kiṣkindhākāṇḍa where Rāma admires the extremely correct language which Māruti speaks. Here perhaps is a reference to the peculiar proficiency of the Dravidian people in grammar and other Śāstras. Now in this eulogy of the grammatical attainments of Māruti in canto XXXVI of the Uttarakāṇḍa this *śloka* in long metre

1. In Gorresio's text we have neither the *śloka* about Buddha nor this which mentions *rāśis*. But the following arguments based on grammatical references as also the interpolated chapter on Rājanīti are to be found therein.

occurs,

स सूत्रवृत्यर्थपदं महार्थं ससंग्रहं सिध्यति वै कपींद्रः ।

The commentator explains सूत्रं अष्टाध्यायीलक्षणम् वृत्तिस्तात्कालिकसूत्रवृत्तिः अर्थपदं सूत्रार्थं बोधकपदवद्वार्तिकम् । महार्थं महाभाष्यं पतञ्जलिकृतं । ससंग्रहं व्याडिकृत-संग्रहाख्य-ग्रंथसहितम् । The above list contains almost all the well-known ancient authors on grammar. Vyāḍi, if the story related in the *Brihat Kathāsaritsāgara* is to be credited, lived in the days of Chandragupta and Nanda and was the teacher of Vararuci. But the reference to Patañjali's *Mahābhāṣya* makes the present edition of the *Rāmāyaṇa* later than the days of Menander whose investment of 'Sāketa' in about 150 B.C. is mentioned by Patañjali in his great work.

We are thus justified on different grounds in placing the higher limit for the compilation of the present *Rāmāyaṇa* in the second century B.C. And here we may note the fact that there are evidences to show that this compilation of the *Rāmāyaṇa* was made after the *Mahābhārata* was put in its present form. We have shown in our first book that the *Mahābhārata* as we have it; dates subsequent to the conquests of Alexander (the Greeks are mentioned by name in that epic with admiration as a very warlike race; the *śloka* in Ādiparva :

न शशाक वशे कर्तुं यं पण्डुरपि वीर्यवान् ।
सोऽर्जुनेन वशं नीतो राजासीद् यवनाधिपः ॥

makes it probable that the exploits of Alexander were fresh in the mind of the last editor of the *Mahābhārata*) but prior to the introduction of *rāśis* about 200 B.C. (for there is no mention of *rāśis* in the *Mahābhārata* at all). Now the present edition of the *Rāmāyaṇa* has copied from the *Mahābhārata* a whole chapter word for word. For, whereas that chapter fits in properly with the context in the *Mahābhārata*, it is an intolerable interpolation in the *Rāmāyaṇa*. The 100th Canto of the Ayodhyākāṇḍa is the same as chapter 5 of the Sabhāparva and treats of the duties of a king and the appliances of good Government. Now Nārada may well ask a hundred questions of Yudhiṣṭhira as to how he governs his kingdom and may well explain to him the ways of best governing it, as the latter is sitting at his ease in the Sabhā doing nothing. But in the *Rāmāyaṇa*, Rāma sees Bharata in a changed form. He already is afraid that their father may be dead and instead of asking him anxious questions as to the news in Ayodhyā, Rāma grows eloquent on the ways of governing a kingdom and puts Bharata who must have governed his kingdom for a week only, a hundred questions which even the reader finds it intolerable to read. But the interpolation of this chapter is proved beyond doubt by the context, for the next canto begins as if the whole of this canto was never there. The beginning *śloka* of the next canto is

तं तु रामः समाज्ञाय भ्रातरं गुरुवत्सलम् ।
लक्ष्मणेन सह भ्रात्रा प्रष्टुं समुपचक्रमे ॥

[knowing him to be fond of his brother, Rāma with his brother Lakṣmaṇa began to ask him]. The words *began to ask him* are significant as they show that nothing had been said before and yet there are a hundred questions put to Bharata in the canto preceding. This proves that the canto is copied by the *Rāmāyaṇa* from the *Mahābhārata* and not vice-versa. Then again Vasudeva is twice mentioned and with reverence in the present *Rāmāyaṇa*. And in the story of the curse of Nimi in the Uttarakāṇḍa there is a direct reference to the Vasudeva of the Yādava family who is to be the next Avatāra. It appears, therefore, clear that the present edition of the *Rāmāyaṇa* is subsequent to the present edition of the *Mahābhārata*, and its date must be somewhere about the first century B.C. In fact in the words of Hunter "while some parts of the *Rāmāyaṇa* are earlier than the *Mahābhārata*, the compilation as a whole belongs to a later date". And here is a clue to the solution of the question why the *Rāmāyaṇa* of Vālmīki was recast.

IV

WHY THE ORIGINAL POEM OF VĀLMĪKI WAS RECAST

The life of Rāma is so pure and exalted that anybody who reads it cannot but feel for him almost divine respect and it is not to be wondered that in India he has always been paid divine honours. Even the Buddhists tried to enlist this national hero of India on their side by transcribing his legend into their own language and by representing him as a former Buddha as is stated at the end of the *Daśaratha Jātaka*. But it appears certain that unlike most great heroes Rāma never claimed for himself divine attributes or divine origin nor did he act in this world as if he were an incarnation of God. As we shall show in another place, it appears that Kṛṣṇa was the first great hero who claimed divinity for himself during his own life-time and was even then looked upon and worshipped as an Avatāra of Viṣṇu. And when Buddha's followers treated him as the Supreme Being and popular sentiment began to conceive of many Buddhas in former times, orthodox Aryans must have found themselves in great danger; for the unreasoning masses always want and cling to, for their mental satisfaction and support, some divine being in human form like Kṛṣṇa or Buddha. The orthodox Aryans, therefore, appear to have at this time generally accepted the doctrine that Vasudeva was an Avatāra of Viṣṇu and thus enlisted the sympathies of an already existing sect in favour of Vedic religion. This necessitated and influenced the re-editing of the *Mahābhārata* in which the whole orthodox Aryan mythology, recast on new lines, was included. National heroes preceding Vasudeva were also represented as former Avatāras of Viṣṇu, in exact imitation of the Buddhists who believed and preached that in every cycle of time Buddha had appeared in one form or another.

In this new representation of the national heroes Rāma who had been taken up even by the Buddhists, was also represented by the Rāmopākhyāna of the *Mahābhārata* as an Avatāra of Viṣṇu. This was the first changed orthodox version of the *Rāmāyaṇa* of Vālmīki and is more archaic than the version of the *Rāmāyaṇa* of to-day, for reasons which we have given elsewhere in this book. The Rāmopākhyāna of the *Mahābhārata* was an incentive to the recasting of the *Rāmāyaṇa* of Vālmīki itself, in accordance with the new theory of Rāma's being an Avatāra of Viṣṇu. And as there was already a model in existence *viz.* the vast re-edition of the *Mahābhārata*, the recasting of the *Rāmāyaṇa* naturally followed the great epic in many other respects also. The *Rāmāyaṇa* of Vālmīki unfortunately fell into the hands of an indifferent editor who could not extend it to the bulk of the *Mahābhārata* nor could cast it in a form which could defy investigation and scrutiny. He could not also imbue the work with that philosophical interest which pre-eminently belongs to the *Mahābhārata* in its present form. The present edition of the *Rāmāyaṇa*, however, still commands our admiration by the force, the imagination, and the simplicity of the original work of Vālmīki which must have impressed and inspired almost completely the modern compiler of it, incompetent as he was in other respects.

Now, owing to this very incompetency of the second compiler, proofs are left to us in the body of the *Rāmāyaṇa* itself which show that the Vaiṣṇavite element did not form part of the original *Rāmāyaṇa* of Vālmīki. This fact has struck almost all persons who have carefully read the poem. Prof. Weber has recorded it as one of the results of his investigation. Prof. Muir has adduced various arguments and proofs in support of the same conclusion in his Sanskrit texts (Appendix to Vol. III) which are, however, not quite sufficient inasmuch as they only go to prové that Rāma acted like a man and invoked Indra and other deities. It may be answered that he was an incarnation in human form and therefore must act like a human being. If he had shown himself and acted as Viṣṇu the whole length of the *Rāmāyaṇa* might have been curtailed by one single wish on his part and Rāvaṇa and Laṅkā might have been annihilated and Sītā got back in a moment. Nay, Rāma could not have been deceived by the golden deer; had he acted like a god and there would have been no abduction of Sītā at all. In fact, the Vedantins lay a great stress on this human conduct of an Avatāra as an essential part of its useful teaching. Many of the *ślokas* quoted by Prof. Muir might be explained away on this theory. But there are some more texts and arguments which in our opinion cannot be thus answered.

Firstly—In the very first canto wherein Nārada gives an account of the exploits of Rāma he says :

दशवर्षसहस्राणि दशवर्षशतानिच ।
रामो राज्यमुपासित्वा ब्रह्मलोकं प्रयास्यति ।।

Now, Rāma should return at the end of his life in this world to the Viṣṇuloka and not to the Brahmaloka. And therefore there is here a clear infringement of the idea of his being an Avatāra of Viṣṇu. For though in his life-time he might act in this world of human beings as other men do, when he leaves this world if he were an Avatāra of Viṣṇu, he should return to Viṣṇuloka. Nārada, therefore, appears to treat Rāma not as an Avatāra of Viṣṇu, but only as a great person who, having lived a meritorious life goes to Brahmaloka after his death. The commentator sees the difficulty created by the *śloka* and explains it thus—

ब्रह्मलोकं मायिकं वैकुण्ठादि लोकम् । अनेन निजनित्यकर्मयोगोपेतस्य ब्रह्मलोकप्राप्तिरिति ध्वनिः ।

"This hints, that whoever performs his necessary religious duties in this life goes to Brahmaloka after death." In the last canto of the Uttarakāṇḍa, however, Brahmā requests Rāma to enter his Vaiṣṇava form or body. Rāma thereupon enters or returns to his own Vaiṣṇava body while his followers, *viz.* the inhabitants of Ayodhyā go to the Santānaka loka, and Sugrīva returns to the Sūrya-maṇḍala or Sun's disc and other monkeys to the bodies of the gods from whose spirit they were generated. It is strange, therefore, that Nārada should not have remembered that Rāma was an Avatāra of Viṣṇu. The words विष्णुना सदृशो वीर्ये used by Nārada in the same canto also go to show that he was not looked upon by Nārada as an incarnation of Viṣṇu. The same expression occurs in many subsequent *sargas* no doubt; and it is possible to explain it to mean by a stretched construction that Rāma was like his counterpart in so far as he lived and acted as a man. Yet even these comparisons would seem ill-placed and unpoetical when the same poet in the same poem tells us that he was an incarnation of Viṣṇu himself.

Secondly—Canto XV of Bālakāṇḍa is the first canto wherein the gods are represented as having repaired to Brahmā and thence to Viṣṇu in order to implore him to incarnate himself as man and destroy the invulnerable Rākṣasa king, Rāvaṇa. Now this canto is so very meagre in detail and description compared with what is found in *Raghuvaṁśa* and the *Padma-purāṇa* and its meagreness is so in contrast with the prolixity and the vivacity of all the other descriptions in the *Rāmāyaṇa* that one cannot but feel that this canto has been subsequently introduced into the body of the work by unskilful hands. Canto XVII relates how the gods knowing that Viṣṇu had created himself as the eldest son of Daśaratha, threw their own *aṁśas* or spirits into the sons of various monkeys in order to assist Rāma. And Indra is said to have taken the form of Vālin. Now Vālin nowhere assists Rāma but on the contrary puts himself in opposition to him. That the most powerful friend and elder brother of Viṣṇu should thus have wasted himself and was of no use to Rāma in his great war with Rāvaṇa, seems to show that the new theory has been somehow fitted on to the already existing *dramatis personæ*.

The theory of the ten Avatāras of Viṣṇu is a creation of the Purāṇas and not of the *Mahābhārata* nor the *Rāmāyaṇa* as is abundantly clear from the *Rāmāyaṇa* itself. The Varāha Avatāra seems not to have been looked upon as an Avatāra of Viṣṇu in the days of the *Rāmāyaṇa*.

ततः समभवद् ब्रह्मा स्वयंभूर्देवतैः सह ।
स वराहस्ततो भूत्वा प्रोज्जहार वसुंधराम् ॥
असृजच्च जगत्सर्वं सह पुत्रैः कृतात्मभिः ॥।

The commentator is in great difficulties over this *śloka* and explains त्रिमूर्त्तेर्विराजः विष्ण्वात्मकोऽंशो वसुंधरां प्रोज्जहार । तस्यैव विराजः रजःप्रधानः सृष्टिव्यापारवानंशो ब्रह्मा इति व्यवह्रियमाणः सर्वं जगत् असृजत् । The Trimūrti and the splitting of ब्रह्मा are, however, all creations of the imagination of the commentator. The plain sense of the text is that "*Brahmā svayaṁbhū* or self-created was born together with the gods. That Brahmā became a Varāha and raised up the earth. He then created this diverse creation together with his blessed sons." From this it clearly appears that it is Brahmā, the Creator who assumed the form of Varāha and not Viṣṇu. The foregoing will sufficiently prove that the modern idea of the 10 Avatāras did not form part of the original *Rāmāyaṇa*. That idea was only in the process of formation at the time of the compilation of the present *Rāmāyaṇa* and developed itself more fully subsequently during the Puranic times. And herein we can also have a chronological data for fixing the date of the compilation of some of the Purāṇas in their present form.

Kālidāsa, like the *Rāmāyaṇa*, represents Rāma as made of one-half of the *aṁśa* or spirit of Viṣṇu while Bharata was made of one-fourth and Lakṣmaṇa and Śatrughna of the remaining one-fourth. The Purāṇas, however, were not satisfied with Rāma being only one-half of Viṣṇu and their theory as given in the *Padma-purāṇa* is that Rāma was a whole Avatāra or full incarnation of Viṣṇu while Bharata was born of the spirit of Pāñcajanya or Viṣṇu's conch, Lakṣmaṇa of the spirit of the great Serpent on which Viṣṇu lies and Śatrughna of the spirit of the Sudarśana Cakra or disc.

कैकेय्यां भरतो जज्ञे पांचजन्यांशसंभवः ।
अनंतांशेन संभूतो लक्ष्मणः परवीरहा ॥
सुदर्शनांशाच्छत्रुघ्नो संजज्ञेऽमितविक्रमः ॥ (*Padma-purāṇa*)

Then again, that the Vaiṣṇavite theory had not completely

formed itself when the *Rāmāyaṇa* was recast, may be seen from the fact that Sītā was identified with a certain Brahmin girl Vedavatī in her former life and not with Lakṣmī, the wife of Viṣṇu. That improvement was made by the *Padma-purāṇa* and the popular belief now is that she was no other than Lakṣmī herself.

अथ लोकेश्वरी लक्ष्मीर्जनकस्य निवेशने ।
सीता मखे समुत्पन्ना बालभावेन सुंदरी ॥

These and other improvements[1] over Kālidāsa himself show that the recompilation of the Purāṇas must have taken place long after Kālidāsa *i.e.*, about the 7th or 8th century A.D.

V

OTHER ADDITIONS MADE IN IMITATION OF THE *MAHĀBHĀRATA*

Having thus shown that the Vaiṣṇavite complexion did not originally belong to the *Rāmāyaṇa* of Vālmīki and that it was recast substantially with a view to its introduction, we may now proceed further to consider the nature of the other additions which must have been made along with this new element, in imitation of the *Mahābhārata* or from other causes. We may first note the additions made by the second

1. We may mention one more instance. It is believed that Lakṣmaṇa ate nothing during his 14 years' residence in the forests as Rāma gave him nothing to eat in order to enable him to obtain so much merit that he might kill Indrajit. This terribly long fast he was enabled to make as he was an Avatāra of Śeṣa, a serpent who lives on air. There is no authority even in the *Rāmāyaṇa* of to-day for such an absurd idea and Lakṣmaṇa is represented as eating flesh freely being served by Sītā along with Rāma. See Ayodhyākāṇḍa—

अग्रे प्रदाय भूतेभ्यः सीताथ वरवर्णिनी ।
तयोरुपददे भ्रात्रोर्मधुमांसं च तद्भुजम् ॥
तयोस्तुष्टिमथोपाद्य वीरयोः कृतजीवयोः ।
निशिथज्ज्ञानकीपश्चात्स्वके तत्राप्यधारणम् ॥

editor of the *Rāmāyaṇa* to allow a free scope to his poetic powers. Thus additional descriptions of the seasons, of the city of Laṅkā, of the magnificence of Rāvaṇa's palace, additional lamentations of Rāma, of Tārā or Sītā, of Kausalyā or Mandodarī and additional conversations between the various actors have in fact nearly doubled the original work. All these interpolations and additions, however, betray themselves by their being almost invariably in long metre sometimes with rhyming lines, by their being a repetition of what already exists in the Anuṣṭubh metre, and very often by the contradiction they involve with what precedes or follows. Take for instance cantos XXII and XXIII of the Ayodhyākāṇḍa with the last part of XXI, *i.e.*, from *śloka* 51 to 64 with long metres. These contain nothing but repetitions in different forms of what has already been stated and the same is the case with *ślokas* 55-61 of canto XXXIV of the Ayodhyākāṇḍa in long metres; so also the whole canto XLI of the same Kāṇḍa is nothing more than a further lamentation but it destroys the context between XL and XLII. So again canto LXIII of the Araṇyakāṇḍa is a fresh lamentation in long metred *ślokas* containing the same idea as have gone before.

Canto XXXI of the Araṇyakāṇḍa relates that Akampana (अकम्पन) went to tell Rāvaṇa of the fight of Rāma with Khara and the death of the latter. Akampana advises Rāvaṇa to abduct Rāma's wife and thus to humble him and destroy his energies. Rāvaṇa, thereafter goes to Mārīci and asks him to assist him in the plan of abduction, but is dissuaded by him and quietly returns to Laṅkā. But this canto destroys the whole beauty of the dexterous manner in which Śūrpaṇakhā suggests to Rāvaṇa the same idea of Sītā's abduction. It forestalls Śūrpaṇakhā's doings and makes the obstinacy of Rāvaṇa appear less fearful and poetic and is a useless anticipation of the same story. That canto XXXI is evidently an interpolation.

Cantos V and VII of the Sundarakāṇḍa contain *ślokas* with rhyming lines and are mere additional descriptions of the rainy-season containing no new beauty. Canto XXVIII also contains *ślokas* with long metres and is a fresh lamentation by Sītā which looks quite out of place. The contradiction and break in the context caused by the interpolation of this canto is very apparent. For canto XXVI contains the bewailings of Sītā when she was frightened by her Rākṣasī attendants. In canto XXVII, Trijaṭā who alone from among the Rākṣasī attendants of Sītā was her friend, tells the Rākṣasīs that she saw a dream in which Rāvaṇa was killed and Rāma was triumphant. Sītā thereupon feels consoled and says in the last *śloka* of canto XXVII—

ततः सा ह्रीमती बाला भर्तुर्विजयहर्षिता ।
अवोचद्यदि तत्सत्यं भवेयं शरणं हि वः ॥

But the first *śloka* in the following canto (XXVIII) reads :

सा राक्षसेंद्रस्य वचो निशम्य तद्रावणस्याप्रियमप्रियार्ता ।
सीता वितत्रास यथा वनान्ते सिंहाबपन्नागजराजकन्या ॥

This reversion again to the words of Rāvaṇa and Sītā's again falling into wailing are wholly incongruous. For after Rāvaṇa's conversation with Sītā and his departure from that place, a great deal has happened *viz.*, the threatening by the Rākṣasīs and Trijaṭā's relation of her dream and Sītā's being comforted. Yet the poet goes on as if Rāvaṇa had just spoken his harsh words to her. A more careful compiler might at least have said अनुस्मृत्य instead of निशम्य. "Sītā recollecting the harsh words of Rāvaṇa" would have been something better than "Sītā on hearing the harsh words." It would be needless to multiply examples of such cantos by whole or parts which have been interpolated simply to increase the bulk of the poem by additional descriptions, lamentations and conversations which become a tiresome reading by their repetition and which more often than not, expose themselves by the contradiction they involve. We will finish this subject by citing one more instance *viz.*, that of canto CXI of the Yuddhakāṇḍa which contains the lamentations of Mandodarī. This canto is not only a repetition of the ideas that have gone before but also involves a clear contradiction. For in canto CX, in *śloka* 23 Vibhīṣaṇa has said to Rāma that he wished to perform the last obsequies of Rāvaṇa's body—

एतस्य यत्प्रेतगतस्य कृत्यं तत्कर्तुमिच्छामि तव प्रसादात् ।

And Rāma assents, remarking—

मरणांतानि वैराणि निर्वृत्तं न प्रयोजनम् ।।

Now, one fails to see why Mandodarī comes in afterwards and laments and why Vibhīṣaṇa reverts to the same subject entertaining quite a different feeling from what he had expressed a little while before. It seems clear that this canto is an interpolation wherein Mandodarī is mentioned for the first and the last time in the *Rāmāyaṇa*. The original poem of Vālmīki, it appears probable, made no mention of Mandodarī, Rāvaṇa's wife, nor of Sulocanā the wife of Indrajit, as we have shown elsewhere, in the same way and with the same poetical beauty as the *Mahābhārata* which nowhere makes a mention of Duryodhana's wife.

1. Allied to this desire of the last compiler to add fresh descriptions, lamentations and conversations to exercise his poetical powers, may be mentioned the desire of still later interpolators to make the *Rāmāyaṇa* a typical *sargabandha kāvya.* It has already been noticed that this alteration in the form of the poem is much later than the last editor as we find the mention of the division of the poem into *adhyāyas* in Bhavabhūti's *Uttararāmacarita.* The desire, however, to make it a perfect *sargabandha kāvya* led to the addition of *ślokas* with long metres at the end of every canto and critics have generally rejected these *ślokas* as spurious. Although in individual instances they may have belonged to the last edition, their obscure metres are generally an index that they are very recent additions. They also generally contain a repetition of ideas and often involve glaring contradictions. One instance will suffice to bring out this subject. In canto LII of the Ayodhyākāṇḍa towards the end we have Rāma saying—

मद्य दुःखं तु वैदेही वनवासस्य वेत्स्यति ।
प्रणष्टजनसंबाधं क्षेत्रारामविवर्जितम् ।।
विषमं च प्रपातं च वनमद्य प्रवेक्ष्यति ।।

And yet in the last added *śloka* in the long metre immediately after we are told—

स लोकपालप्रतिमप्रभावस्तीर्त्वा महात्मा वरदो महानदीम् ।
ततः समृद्धान् शुभसस्यमालिनः क्षणेन वत्सान् मुदितानुपागमत् ॥

As a matter of fact the prosperous country of the Vatsas had no existence in the days of Rāma and the whole region between the Yamuna and the Ganges was a great jungle without habitation or settlement except that of Bhāradvāja at the confluence of the two great rivers.

2. An equally great scope for interpolations and additions lay in the matter of legends. After the recasting of the *Mahābhārata* it probably became the ambition of every great epic and the Purāṇa to make it the depository of legends. And we find in the *Rāmāyaṇa* of to-day hundreds of legends told both in place and out of place. The largest additions in the form of legends are to be found in the Uttarakāṇḍa. Not satisfied with the already long history of Rāvaṇa's exploits and misdeeds as given in the Uttarakāṇḍa, cantos are being constantly added which the commentators themselves threw out as spurious. The legends about Vālin and Māruti found in the Uttarakāṇḍa are probably later additions and particularly the reference to Māruti's grammatical attainments. But further on we find very many legends put into the mouth of Lakṣmaṇa who tells various stories about sacrifices to Rāma who in turn relates various stories to Lakṣmaṇa. The second compiler has certainly betrayed his unskilfulness in representing Lakṣmaṇa as relating stories to Rāma. Usually it is the older and more respected person who tells stories. And yet in cantos LXXXIV and LXXXV of Uttarakāṇḍa, we have the strange spectacle of the younger and less experienced Lakṣmaṇa relating legendary stories to Rāma. In fact Rāma's asking Lakṣmaṇa to tell him the well-known story of Vṛttra's destruction sounds absurd and laughable. The last editor, however, wished to bring in all or as many current legends as he could and put them in the mouth of one or other actor indiscriminately.

It would be long if we were to go over the whole length

of the *Rāmāyaṇa*, and discuss which legends appear to have been interpolated under this head. Nor is this subject very easy. But a few examples might be given which would show how some of the legends added, betray themselves. The story of Śāntā and Ṛṣyaśṛṅga is an addition, for that story evidently cuts the context. Daśaratha tells his preceptor Vasiṣṭha of his desire to perform an Aśvamedha and he approves of the idea and tells the king to prepare a sacrificial ground on the other bank of Sarayū and to let go the sacrificial horse. Daśaratha even directs his queens to enter on the vow or *dīkṣā* and they are all glad. Then interposes Sumanta, a wiser man perhaps than Vasiṣṭha, and tells strange stories about Sanatkumāra and eventually Ṛṣyaśṛṅga is brought. And then there is the same question by the king to the Ṛṣis and Vasiṣṭha and the same answer and the same directions by the king to his ministers.

संभाराः सम्भ्रियंतां ते तुरगश्च विमुच्यताम् ।
सरय्वाश्चोत्तरे तीरे यज्ञभूमिर्विधीयताम् ॥

is thus thrice repeated. In short, this legend seems to have been interposed subsequently as it clearly breaks the context. The legends about the quarrels between Viśvāmitra and Vasiṣṭha are again of this sort. They are related by Śatānanda who waxes eloquent on the wonderful deeds of Viśvāmitra while everybody is willing to hear more of the original story. These stories were no doubt copied from the *Mahābhārata* and there are other indications of their being re-touched which will be noticed further on.

The second Kāṇḍa is peculiarly free from legends and so also the third. The story of the crow and its eye having been struck through is interpolated (प्रक्षिप्त) and the commentators have not commented on it. But this addition seems to have been made even before Bhavabhūti for his famous *śloka* in the *Uttararāmacarita* is taken from this interpolated canto

त्वदर्थमिव विन्यस्तः शिलापट्टोऽयमग्रतः ।
यस्यायमभितः पुष्पैः प्रवृष्ट इव केसरः ॥

This canto is also against the chaste tenour of the *Rāmā*-

yaṇa wherein the loves of Rāma and Sītā are described in the purest and the most inoffensive manner. The story of Vātāpi and Ilvala is also interpolated, for here too we have a break in the context and a repetition of *ślokas*. The following *śloka* is twice repeated—

निगृह्य तरसा मृत्युं लोकानां हितकाम्यया ।
यस्य भ्रात्रा कृतेयं दिक् शरण्या पुण्यकर्मणा ॥

Herein is also used the word Sanskrit as denoting the Aryan language, a name which is not found in earlier works—धारयन् ब्राह्मणं रूपमिल्वलः संस्कृतं वदन् । There are some interpolated legends in the Kiṣkindhākāṇḍa, but very few in the Sundara and the Yuddhakāṇḍa; the greatest number is, as has been said above, found in the Uttarakāṇḍa and many of these are plainly interpolated.

3. Another source of amplification was the natural desire of the last editor to make the *Rāmāyaṇa* a depository of knowledge as of legend. The *Mahābhārata* undoubtedly excels every other work in this respect. There we have the principles of Daṇḍanīti, (government) of Rājanīti (politics) of philosophy and ethics, of science and religion detailed with a fulness which may not be found even in many a separate work on each of these subjects. The *Bhagavadgītā* and the Śānti and Anuśāsana-parvas are now regular authorities in matters—philosophical and religious. The last editor of the *Rāmāyaṇa* was greatly at a disadvantage in this respect; perhaps the nature of the work as it already existed did not afford sufficient opportunity for the display of his knowledge or he was not skilful or learned enough Yet in imitation of the great epic long *sargas* are here and there interposed, treating of the various branches of knowledge,—*sargas* which betray their spurious nature by their inconsistency. The 100th canto of the Ayodhyākāṇḍa where Rāma preaches to his brother the science of government at a time when he should have been anxiously inquiring about the events in Ayodhyā, has already been shown not only to be a copy word for word of a chapter in the *Mahābhārata* but also as inconsistent with the context.

In Kiṣkindhākāṇḍa cantos XL to XLIV, the last editor makes a similar mess by making Sugrīva tell his search parties, the geography of the world. The discrepancy between the previous statement of Sugrīva that he did not know the abode of the evil Rākṣasa (Rāvaṇa) and his subsequent statement that Laṅkā was the abode of that evil Rākṣasa who deserved to be killed, has already been noticed. But there are other glaring inconsistencies in this geographical interpolation. In the first place the geography as given in Kiṣkindhākāṇḍa strangely enough takes for its centre a point somewhere near Delhi and not Kiṣkindhā from where Sugrīva is giving his directions. Thus countries and rivers which lie to the north of Kiṣkindhā are mentioned as lying in the southern direction. In fact the unskilful compiler has copied, without the necessary changes, the description of the world as found in some work which naturally took for its centre, Kurukshetra, the centre of the Aryan world. The commentator sees the difficulty and remarks—हिमवद्विन्ध्यमध्यवर्ति आर्यावर्तापेक्षया प्राच्यादिविभागाः. Another grave inconsistency is the mention of the Pāṇḍyas by Sugrīva in this geography of the world—युक्तं कवाटं पांड्यानां गता द्रक्ष्यथ वानराः. Now had the Pāṇḍyas been in existence at that time and other Aryan nations of the south mentioned in other places[1] it is strange that Rāma was in so great a difficulty about obtaining human aid in finding out Sītā and fighting with Rāvaṇa. It cannot be doubted that at the time of Rāma there were no Aryan settlements to the south of the Godāvarī. The mention of the Pāṇḍyas is, therefore, simply anachronous. The Pāṇḍyas were well-known in the days of the Greeks and it is no wonder that the compiler who recast the *Rāmāyaṇa* about 100 B.C. should have mentioned them in copying the geography of the world as then known, word for word. A further discrepancy arising from this geographical interpolation may be found in the fact that while in Araṇya-

1. The following princes attended Rāma's intended coronation—प्राच्याः सिंधुसौवीराः सौराष्ट्राः दाक्षिणात्याः । २७ । १० । २. This is evidently a later interpolation for the reasons set forth above.

kāṇḍa we find the Āśrama of Agastya situate on the northern bank of the Godāvarī, we find here the Āśrama of the same sage on the top of the Malaya hill.

तस्यासीनं नगस्याग्रे मलयस्य महौजसः ।
द्रक्ष्यथादित्यसंकाशमगस्त्यमृषिसत्तमम् ॥

The commentator explains that Agastya had many Āśramas. But the fact seems to be that Agastya had been shifted in popular belief further south and when the description borrowed by the compiler was written, Agastya had probably that position assigned to him. And the compiler took the description as it was; without caring to see the contradiction involved.

4. The last though not the least motive for the expansion of the *Rāmāyaṇa* seems to have been the wish to exaggerate the marvellous. We have already adverted to the fact that that yearning for the marvellous has not yet been satisfied and is constantly adding to the number of miracles and wonders in Rāma's life so much so that by the side of what people believe at present even the last orthodox edition of the *Rāmāyaṇa* seems simple and prosaic. The same yearning for the marvellous must have induced the last editor to expand or invent; he might at least have incorporated such stories as had gained credence amongst the people by his time. Such additions also sometimes betray themselves by the contradictions they involve, contradictions which the last editor has left intact probably owing to his oversight, perhaps owing to his desire to keep the poem of Vālmīki as it was. Take for instance the story of the golden deer with jewelled eyes. This beautiful story appears not to have been a part of the original *Rāmāyaṇa*. Most probably Rāma and Lakṣmaṇa had both inadvertently gone out a-hunting confiding Sītā to the care of Jaṭāyu.[1] And Rāvaṇa taking

1. Jaṭāyu's saying to Rāma—

सोऽहं वाससहायस्ते भविष्यामि यदीच्छसि ।
सीतां च तात रक्षिष्ये त्वयि याते सलक्ष्मणे ॥

is here very relevant.

advantage of the rare opportunity must have abducted her after slaying Jaṭāyu. Had Rāma gone after a golden deer and Lakṣmaṇa followed him on hearing a cry of distress, Sītā would not have said to Rāvaṇa. "Please wait, my husband will soon return taking with him plenty of forest fruit and the flesh of many a deer, porcupines and boars."

आगमिष्यति मे भर्ता वन्यमादाय पुष्कलम् ।
रुरून् गोधान् वराहांश्च हत्वादायामिषं बहु ॥

It cannot be urged that she is telling herein what she hoped to see for she might have told him that her husband had gone after a golden deer, with the same simplicity and truthfulness with which she had related her whole story. Then again, the story is somewhat inconsistent and inartistic at the point where Rāvaṇa is introduced as a devotee and Sītā without any suspicion speaks to him as if nothing had happened before between her and her brother-in-law. For the latter had told her that there was no fear for Rāma and that it was merely a trick played by the artful Rākṣasas; and she had spoken to him such harsh words as she would never have used but in an agony of feelings; but strangely enough it leaves no trace behind when Rāvaṇa appears. To our mind the story of the golden deer is somewhat faulty and unsustainable and one would rather believe from what Sītā said in the couplet quoted above that Rāma and Lakṣmaṇa had merely gone out on an ordinary hunting and fruit-collecting expedition confiding her to Jaṭāyu.

The story of Śarabhaṅga and Indra's *vimāna* of heavenly splendour hanging before his hermitage appears again dubious. And Rāma gives the same answer in reply to the same question by Śarabhaṅga and Sutīkṣṇa in Araṇyakāṇḍa

अहमेवाहरिष्यामि स्वयं लोकान्महामुने ।
आवासं त्वहमिच्छामि प्रदिष्टमिह कानने ॥ V.36

This *śloka* is also curious in another way. In the first half, Rāma exhibits a consciousness of his being Viṣṇu or God himself and in the very next breath he exhibits his human frailty and asks for information. The *śloka* is also inconsistent with the following *śloka* in the next *adhyāya*—

आपृच्छाम: प्रयास्यामो मुनयस्त्वरयंति न: ।
त्वरामहे वयं द्रष्टुं कृत्स्नमाश्रममंडलम् ॥

A great many other marvellous stories may be mentioned which appear on the face of them to be subsequent additions by their very exaggeration and needlessness. The story of the wonderful feast given by Bharadvāja to Bharata's army with the aid of his miraculous powers is an unnecessary repetition of the feast given by Vasiṣṭha to Viśvāmitra's army. The story of the dead Daśaratha appearing before Rāma in canto CIXX of Yuddhakāṇḍa is an interpolation made in imitation of the *Mahābhārata* where the dead heroes of the great war rise before the survivors as they pour libations of the water of Ganges in their name. This story in the *Rāmāyaṇa* is not wanted by the context and has no dramatic or moral effect. The story of Māruti's bringing the Droṇa hill from the Himalaya is thrice repeated and one would think that when once brought, the hill might have been retained in the camp to obviate the necessity of its being brought again and again. The story of Garuḍa coming to raise Rāma from the *sarpabandha* of Indrajit is plainly an interpolation, for in the very previous canto Rāma is said to have risen from his swoon by his own great strength and vitality—

तावुत्थाप्य महातेजा गरुडो वासवोपमौ ।
उभौ च सस्वजे हृष्टो रामश्चैनमुदीक्षत ॥

is plainly opposed to—

एतस्मिन्नंतरे राम: प्रत्यबुध्यत वीर्यवान् ।
स्थिरत्वात्सत्वयोगाच्च शरै: संदानितोऽपि सन् ॥

The story of the appearance of all the gods headed by Brahmā when Sītā performs her ordeal, is again an addition, for Agni has already proclaimed the purity of Sītā. Strangely enough Rāma asks the gods who he was and Brahmā then enters on a *stuti* in the usual Vedantic strain. One fails to see the relevancy of the question of Rāma to the general tenour of the story. It would be tedious to the reader to detail other stories added in order to increase the marvellous element in the *Rāmāyaṇa*. They are to be found throughout the whole length of the poem and many stories strike even a casual reader as interpolations and additions. In fact, the *Rāmāyaṇa* of Vālmīki himself must have made a large stand on this figure of speech *viz.* *atiśayokti* or hyperbole and every later compilation or editing tended to increase this striking feature of the poem. We will finish this part by adducing one more glaring instance of this kind of exaggeration.

The original *Rāmāyaṇa* like the Vedas represented the lives of men as not inordinately long, not longer than the limit given by the Vedic line शतायुर्वै पुरुषः. Rāma, married at 16 or 18, an age which need not be wondered at in connection with a Kṣatriya prince of exhuberant growth and powerful frame; was to be invested with the power of the heir apparent at 28 or 30 but was sent into exile; conquered Laṅkā, returned to Ayodhyā and was installed in his rightful place at 42 a course of life not much differing from the ordinary run of human life. And yet with indigestible exaggeration it is represented that Rāma thereafter reigned for 11,000 years. Daśaratha is represented to have reigned 60,000 years though Daśaratha himself curiously enough admits that the ordinary length of a human life was 100 years.

प्राप्य वर्षसहस्राणि बहून्यायूंषि जीवतः ।

The commentator explains बहून्यायूंषि by वत्सरशतरूपाण्यनेकपुरुषायूंषि. It is really absurd that Daśaratha should alone have lived 60,000 years while men about him lived ordinarily for 100 years. This feature of fabulously long lives introduced by the last editor has been made still more ridiculous by the absurd story of a Brahmin's son dying prematurely, as introduced in Uttarakāṇḍa. This prematurely deceased child was only 5000 years old and had not yet attained boyhood.

अप्राप्तयौवनं बालं पंचवर्षसहस्रकम् ।
अकाले कालमापन्नं मम दुःखाय पुत्रकम् ॥

The commentator no doubt explains the absurdity by saying that "years" here meant "days." But this use of the word "year" is certainly unwarranted. And why should we not understand the word in the same sense when it is said that Rāma ruled 11,000 years or that Daśaratha 60,000? Yet Kālidāsa has followed the above idea in its literal sense when he says वर्षाणामयुतं ययौ ।

A similar fabulous elongation of life is introduced in the life of Vasiṣṭha with the same result *viz.* that there is a hopeless contradiction. Where Vasiṣṭha recites in the true *kṣatriya* fashion the genealogy of Rāma at the time of his marriage, he says about Sagara

द्वे चास्य भार्ये गर्भिण्यौ बभूवतुरिति श्रुतिः ।

"*There is a tradition* that he (Sagara) had two wives who became pregnant." A similar expression is used in the 100th canto of Ayodhyākāṇḍa

कल्माषपादपुत्रोऽभूच्छंखणस्त्विति नः श्रुतम् ।

"We have *heard* that Kalmāṣapāda had a son named Śankhaṇa." This proves that Vasiṣṭha did not exist in the days of either Sagara or Kalmāṣapāda. In another canto of Ayodhyākāṇḍa he says स तेऽहं पितुराचार्यस्तव चैव परंतप । Probably this Vasiṣṭha was the preceptor of Daśaratha and his son only. Now the belief at the time of the last editor was, as it has been ever since, that one Vasiṣṭha lived for ages and was the preceptor of the Ikṣvāku race from the beginning down to Rāma. Accordingly in the interpolated legends about Vasiṣṭha and Viśvāmitra, we find him to be the preceptor of त्रिशंकु who according to the genealogy given by Vasiṣṭha himself at the time of the marriage; was the seventh ancestor of the father of Sagara,

त्रिशंकुरिति विख्यातः इक्ष्वाकुकुलवर्धनः ।
वसिष्ठं स समाहूय कथयामास चिंतितम् ॥

Then again we have—

इक्ष्वाकूणां हि सर्वेषां पुरोधाः परमा गतिः ।

It is possible to explain that the Vasiṣṭha family and not the same Vasiṣṭha acted as the *purohitas* of the Ikṣvāku family. But the popular belief does not accept this solution and we have the contradiction that whereas Vasiṣṭha in one place says he had *heard* about Sagara, in another he is represented as the preceptor of Sagara's 8th ancestor.

Before finishing this chapter we must refer to and try to solve the extremely difficult question whether the Uttarakāṇḍa as a whole is an interpolation or whether any portion of it was written by the original author. That the bulk of it is as old as the last editor of the 1st century B.C. is unquestioned, for Kālidāsa gives the story of Uttarakāṇḍa in the very same form and often in the very same words. Kālidāsa's cantos on their face appear to be an abstract made of the Uttarakāṇḍa in its present form. But the question is whether the Uttarakāṇḍa is as old as Vālmīki. The fact that the Yuddhakāṇḍa ends with the usual benedictions which indicate the *finis* of a poem, does not solve the question. For, the very name and context of the Uttarakāṇḍa shows it to be an admittedly subsequent volume. It is an Uttara or after-kāṇḍa and the context shows that the poem as it ends with the Yuddhakāṇḍa was recited by Rāma's sons Kuśa and Lava before him and therefore, the fact of the recital of the events which led to it and the events which happened after it, could not properly come in the poem itself. But the following would lead us to think that the nucleus of the Uttarakāṇḍa, subsequent as it is, must have been written by the original author himself. *Firstly*, the history and greatness of Rāvaṇa required to be detailed somewhere, for without them the poem would have been incomplete and the greatness of Rāma without a strong relief. *Secondly*, the painful sequal of the recital of the poem *viz.*, the disappearance of Sītā has so beautifully been conceived that even if the incidents were supposed to be imaginary none but the great poet himself could have conceived them. In fact, they strike us as a part and parcel of the grand tragedy of the epic.

The Uttarakāṇḍa has unquestionably been the subject of the greatest number of additions and interpolations and is being added to even till now. Cantos after cantos have been rejected by commentators as spurious. A great contradiction exists in the story related as to why Rāvaṇa was prevented from forcibly ravishing Sītā. The story of a curse given by Nalakubera (as related in the Uttarakāṇḍa) is diametrically opposed to the story of a curse by Brahmā himself (as given in canto XIII of the Yuddhakāṇḍa) for Rāvaṇa's rape on Punjikasthalā. Such contradictions noticed even by the commentators often puzzle the critic and it is difficult to say whether the one or the other or both are subsequent additions. The Bhaviṣya portion of the Uttarakāṇḍa, *viz.*, that portion which relates to events subsequent to the disappearance of Sītā, appears to be entirely a later addition. The forms of verbs curiously enough are not in the future tense. It seems inexplicable why past tense forms are used when the last editor intended this portion to present what Vālmīki foretold of the future life of Rāma. This foretelling again is opposed to what has been said in the beginning of the first Kāṇḍa. There by a boon from Brahmā, Vālmīki perfectly knew what had happened before.

पुरायत्तत्र निर्वृत्तं पाणावामलकं यथा ।

Herein Vālmīki does not lay claim to know the future but only the past. But the commentator contrives to make the Bhaviṣya portion consistent by remarking यन्निर्वृत्तं जातं इदमुपलक्षणं यच्च भावि । "The past includes the future". No doubt, the Bhaviṣya portion is a natural complement of the epic. The reader is curious to know what becomes of Rāma and his twin sons, of Lakṣmaṇa and Bharata, of Māruti and Sugrīva and the other actors in the epic. As the Odyssey is a natural complement of the *Iliad* which does not say what became of Troy and its siege, of Paris and Helen, of Ulysses and Agamemnon so the Bhaviṣya portion and even the Uttarakāṇḍa as a whole, is a natural complement of the story of the *Rāmāyaṇa*. The Bhaviṣya *Rāmāyaṇa*, however, strikes us as more imaginary than real. It consists chiefly of stories related by Rāma to Lakṣmaṇa and by Lakṣmaṇa to Rāma. It refers to the founding of kingdoms by the sons of Rāma, Lakṣmaṇa, Bharata and Śatrughna, kingdoms which were well-known in the time of the last editor. It appears probable that the various ruling races of India of that day must have invented these stories in order to connect themselves with the celebrated sun-race of Ayodhyā, a family exalted above others by the birth of Rāma, the incarnation of Viṣṇu.

RÉSUMÉ

The various reasons which must have led to the expansion of the old *Rāmāyaṇa* of Vālmīki appear to be (*i*) the theory of Rāma being an Avatāra of Viṣṇu borrowed from the *Mahābhārata;* (*ii*) the theory that the *Rāmāyaṇa* was the first *sargabandhakāvya;* (*iii*) poetical embellishment, or the desire to put in more descriptions of seasons, battles, cities and palaces and more lamentations, eulogies and dialogues; (*iv*) the desire to make the *Rāmāyaṇa* a depository of legendary lore; (*v*) the desire to make it a depository of knowledge; and (*vi*) the desire to exaggerate the marvellous. If we take off the accretions that have gathered about the old *Rāmāyaṇa* of Vālmīki from these various causes we shall have left behind a residuum which even in its simple march of events is extremely interesting and what is more, beautifully sublime in its moral teaching as we will show in the next chapter. We have now an idea as to when, why and to what extent the old nucleus of the *Rāmāyaṇa* of Vālmīki was recast substantially, in a form which, though since then varying within narrow limits, has been handed down to us in a nearly permanent condition. As a natural consequence in that extended form two states of society and civilization, of feeling and aspirations, of knowledge and belief are reflected side by side often in obvious contradiction. For two potent causes had intervened between the original *Rāmāyaṇa* and its subsequent amplification, causes which had convulsed and changed society *viz.*, the rise and progress of Buddhism and the contact with Western civilization brought in the train of the conquests of Alexander. We thus find Kausalyā slaying the sacrificial horse with her own hands and Sītā taking charge of the deer killed by Rāma and Lakṣmaṇa and preparing a flesh repast for the brothers side by side with the obviously incongruous tirade against animal-slaughter put into the mouth of Sītā herself (see canto IX, Ayodhyākāṇḍa). We find men and women alike engaged in the performance of Vedic rites such as *sandhyā* and sacrifice and yet we find the mention of temples as they must have existed after the introduction of Buddhism in the land and city of Ayodhyā. The luxurious palaces of the city of Ayodhyā, the march of Bharata with his grand army, the public temples and gardens are described with a gorgeousness which reminds us of the splendour of the great kings of Magadha and yet we find Rāma, Lakṣmaṇa and Sītā walking bare-footed through the streets of Ayodhyā and willing and able to pass 14 years in the wilderness depending on their own labour and prowess for their subsistence and protection. Again we find Daśaratha and Janaka, Rāma and Lakṣmaṇa constantly guiding their conduct by referring to the conjunctions of the moon and the fixed stars, for the Vedic Aryans knew only the fixed stars and the path of the moon among them and knew not the signs of the Zodiac or the *rāśis*. And yet the births of Rāma and his brothers are, according to later astrology borrowed from the Greeks, recorded by the position of the planets among the various signs. It is in short difficult to deny that the *Rāmāyaṇa* as it exists to-day, consists of an old nucleus written by Vālmīki before the rise of Buddhism, buried in substantial additions made, long after the invasion of Alexander, about the 1st century B.C.

There is in our opinion an admission in the poem itself to this effect. We find it stated शृणोति य इदं काव्यं पुरा वाल्मीकिना कृतम् and at another place आदिकाव्यमिदं चार्षं पुरा वाल्मीकिना कृतम् in the last canto of the Yuddhakāṇḍa. Now it is impossible to explain the word पुरा without supposing that the poem as it was formerly composed by Vālmīki, was subsequently re-touched and expanded. The word पुरा is indeed inconsistent with the theory that the poem as it is, was composed by Vālmīki and sung by his pupils before

Rāma. Nor it is possible to explain the word पुरा by saying that the poem was composed by Vālmīki long before Rāma's birth for even the *Rāmāyaṇa* in its present form does not lay claim to having been prophesied. In short, the word पुरा clearly betrays itself. The poem is also described to be, like the original poem of Vyāsa, an old history पूजयंश्च पठंश्चैनमितिहासं पुरातनम् । and again दिव्यमार्षस्तवं चैनमितिहासं पुरातनम् ॥ (युद्धकाण्ड). The words "old history" also show the same thing, for they cannot be used by Vālmīki himself especially when the poem was to be recited by Rāma's sons before him. They were used by the last editor, when he recast the poem in its present form, in this finishing benediction probably failing to see that they would be inconsistent with the supposition that the poem as it was, was composed by Vālmīki himself.

VI

THE *RĀMĀYAṆA* AS AN EPIC POEM

Divested of its accretions and exhuberances, the *Rāmāyaṇa* of Vālmīki has undoubtedly one of the most fascinating and at the same time most elevating poems that have ever been written in any language.[1] It is in passion and in imagination that the *Rāmāyaṇa* towers over all other Sanskrit poems. If the *Mahābhārata* teaches you the lessons of life, the *Rāmāyaṇa* preaches the highest ideals of it. If one describes the troubles and the turmoils of this real world, the other delineates the pleasures and the pains of an imaginary sublime life. In short, to one who delights in the ethereal and the stupendous, the elevating and the sublime, the *Rāmāyaṇa* of Vālmīki is one of the ideal poems of the world. Indeed it has always been looked upon as the first and the foremost Mahākāvya in

1. It is indeed so charming and sublime that it has been translated into most of the foreign languages *e.g.*, by Faizi into Persian, by Griffith into English and others.

Sanskrit literature. Perhaps the very definition of a Mahākāvya has been in India evolved from this first and superb type of it, as in Western poetics the definition of an epic poem has been evolved from the *Iliad*. A Mahākāvya according to Sanskrit poeticians ought to contain descriptions of the seasons, of sunset and sunrise, of cities and forests, of the march of armies and battles, etc.[1] The *Rāmāyaṇa* contains most splendid descriptions of these and has served as a model to later Sanskrit poets in the composition of their Mahākāvyas.

But if the *Rāmāyaṇa* is a Mahākāvya according to Sankrit poetics, judged by Western standards, it is not an epic poem though it is usually classed as such. Its subject is not one great complex action nor is it told in language dignified and stately. Properly speaking it is a mixture of heroic and lyric poetry. It records the great actions of an individual hero, and is told in rapid impassioned verse. Arnold observes "Lyrical poetry as its name denotes, implied originally that the words were accompanied by lively music; a rapid movement and corresponding rapidity in the verse which are essential to it. It is the glowing utterance of minds not calm and thoughtful but excited and impassioned." Now in the very beginning of the *Rāmāyaṇa* we are told that Vālmīki having composed his poem on the exploits of Rāma and the sublime life of Sītā looked about for some one to sing it and his eyes fell on Kuśa and Lava, the cast-away sons of Rāma. He taught them to sing the poem to the accompaniment of a stringed instrument. The boys whose names combined have become synonymous with singers, sang the impassioned poem to the delight of its hearers. We have thus the evidence of the author himself that his poem is more lyrical than epic. We will, however, criticise it in the usual fore-fold aspects

१. संध्यासूर्येन्दुरजनीप्रदोषध्वान्तवासराः । प्रातर्मध्याह्नमृगयाशैलर्तुवनसागराः ।
संभोगविप्रलंभौ च मुनिस्वर्गपुराध्वराः । रणप्रयाणोपयममंत्रपुत्रोदयादयः ॥
वर्णनीया यथायोगं सांगोपांगा अमी इह ॥

—साहित्यदर्पण

of an epic poem, *viz.*, the fables, the characters, the sentiments and the language.

The subject of the *Rāmāyaṇa* is well suited for a lyric poem. Rāma's life though not as varied and full of incidents as the life of the Pāṇḍavas, is yet the life of a hero who lived an ideally sublime life. Indeed of all the heroes who have been deified by the nations of antiquity, Rāma stands pre-eminently at the head as having lived a life singularly pure and noble. With the exception of one act there is not a single spot in his career on which one can lay finger as evidencing the working of a mind influenced by earthly much less sordid motives. The life of Rāma has for thousands of years held the Hindu mind in subjection by its purity and nobleness and it is probable that it will do so for years to come. It is a life well fitted to raise emotions of the highest order—emotions which lyric poetry loves to deal with, such as devotion, loyalty, love and heroism. There is another charm in the life of Rāma inasmuch as it has a pathos which is seldom found in any invented or real story. Throughout the whole of Rāma's life runs a vein of noble suffering which rouses not our pity but our admiration mixed with a feeling of pain. Addison has observed—"There are two kinds of implex fables. In the first, the chief actor makes his way through a long series of dangers and difficulties until he arrives at honour and prosperity as we see in the story of Ulysses. In the second, the chief actor falls from some eminent pitch of honour into misery and disgrace. Thus we see Adam and Eve sinking from a state of innocence into the most abject condition of sin and sorrow. This kind of an implex fable wherein the end is unhappy, is more apt to affect an audience than that of the first kind." Now it may be questioned whether this division of the implex fable is complete. There are fables which though do not end in the dishonour and disgrace of the hero which is really not a good thing, end in something untoward which, however, does not lower the hero in our estimation. He has done all that could be done by man and yet in the end is unhappy. Such is the story of Rāma. Rāvaṇa was conquered and killed and Sītā recovered. She went through the ordeal of fire-purification and yet she had to be abandoned when Rāma came back to Ayodhyā, in consequence of popular disapprobation. And when again she came back with her sons under Vālmīki's escort, she disappeared in the womb of her mother earth. It is an exquisite tragic turn which the poet has given to the story. The story of *Mahābhārata* is equally tragic in the end; for the triumph of the Pāṇḍavas was turned into a disaster by the night surprise of their camp by the unscrupulous Aśvatthāmā, and in the morning Draupadī fell insensible at the sight of her sons and brothers murdered in cold blood, and Yudhiṣṭhira could only exclaim "the conquerors have themselves been conquered owing to their negligence."

Though the stories of the *Rāmāyaṇa* and the *Mahābhārata* are thus equally exquisitely tragic, the characters in the two poems differ most essentially. The actors in Vyāsa's epic, elevated as they are, strike us as real beings; the actors in the *Rāmāyaṇa* are ethereal. They do not touch this earth but seem to move above it. It is related in the *Mahābhārata* that Yudhiṣṭhira's chariot moved above the ground but when he uttered the only lie he had told in his life the chariot touched the earth. This is only a poetic way of describing the greatness of Yudhiṣṭhira's stainless character. He seemed to walk above the ground unsoiled by the infirmities of this human world. Like the one Yudhiṣṭhira in the *Mahābhārata* the characters in the *Rāmāyaṇa* one and all seem to move in an ethereal sphere. We have in the *Rāmāyaṇa* the most affectionate father, the most cruel step-mother, the most dutiful son, the most loving husband, the most devoted wife, the most faithful friend and the most uncompromising enemy. The characters of Rāma and Sītā tower above all, the sublimest that have ever been conceived. Rāma is everything that is noble as a son or a brother or a friend or a king. His love for his subjects and the care he took of them, have become proverbial and the word "Rāma-rājya" has become synonymous with a benign and happy rule. Even the *Mahābhārata* contains praises of Rāma's rule which is everywhere represented as a millennium. And who can sufficiently describe the beauty of the character which the father of Sanskrit poetry has conceived and delineated in the person of Sītā ? The poet has succeeded in evolving an ideal woman placed in an ineffably sacred atmosphere. Her name is in the mind of a Hindu surrounded by the most hallowed ideas and she is a heavenly embodiment of all that a wife should be.

The sentiments which the poet has put in the mouth of his actors are such as sustain the ideal characters which he has assigned to them. There is not a single sentiment which breathes any thing but the highest feelings. It is not possible to give here many instances of such noble sentiments with regard to each character; we will only give some of the noble utterances of Sītā. When Rāma tries to dissuade her from accompanying him to the forest, full of dangers and difficulties as it was, she says, "I will walk in front of thee crushing the thorns and the pointed grass (for thy sake)." "I love to roam in the jungles for are they not full of sweet scents ?" As Bhavabhūti has observed when taking up the above line from the *Rāmāyaṇa*.

त्वया सह निवत्स्यामि वनेषु मधुगंधिषु ।
इति हा रमते सीता स्नेहस्तस्याः स तादृशः ।।

"It is indeed unbounded love which made Sītā think so." When she was abandoned in the forest again after her return to Ayodhyā by Lakṣmaṇa she sent a message to Rāma which every time that you read it, moves you to tears. In the 13th canto of *Raghuvaṁśa*, Kālidāsa repeats the same well-known message of Sītā and adds an exquisite finishing touch of his own. "I will perform penance," says Sītā, "when the fœtus in my womb has been delivered, in order that I may have thee again in my next life as my husband, but no separation from thee as in this." The oath which Sītā takes when Vālmīki brings her before Rāma and the long suffering queen with the instinct of a woman suddenly resolves to put an end to her life, is the noblest that has ever been conceived. "If I have not wronged my husband by deeds, words or even thoughts, let goddess Earth take me into her bosom."

मनसा कर्मणा वाचा यथा रामं समर्चये ।
तथा मे माधवी देवी विवरं दातुमर्हति ।।[1]

Indeed Sītā's devotion and chastity have been the life-springs which have fed the mute love and contentment so characteristic of Hindu wives for these thousands of years. Vālmīki is almost unsurpassed in the development of pathos. Tragic poetry attempts to carry our feelings to the highest point of sublime pathos, so much so that we feel ourselves enchanted by the very intensity of our pain. Like the natural phenomenon of two opposites meeting each other when intensified, our highly wrought feeling of pain finally merges into a feeling of pleasure. The Ayodhyākāṇḍa furnishes many illustrations of this highly intensified pathos. We may take for instance the scene wherein Kaikeyī catching Rāma at his word placed before him and his brother and wife garments of bark which they were to wear and depart in exile. Inexperienced Sītā unable to wear her garment was puzzled, and in her anguish asked her husband "how do wives of anchorites wear bark garments." There she stood aimlessly handling the garment about her neck and looking as if she would swoon every moment. The scene was so painful that it drew tears from the eyes of the ladies of the family and they all cried with one voice. "Rāma, do not take Sītā to the forest. The blessed princess cannot live in a jungle." Rāma, however, ran to her rescue and heedless of their words tied the garment over her silken sari.

Powerful and sublime as Vālmīki is in the delineation of ideal human characters and the development of pathos, he is unsurpassed by any Sanskrit poet in the description of natural scenery. The six seasons of India have been most eloquently described by Vālmīki in several books

1. *Cf.* Kālidāsa —वाङ्मनः कर्मभिः पत्युर्व्यभिचारो यथा न मे ।
तथा विश्वंभरे देवि मामंतर्धातुमर्हसि ।।

of his poem. Modern Sanskrit poetry, we may venture to remark, contains very few descriptions of natural scenery; and those that exist, are full of artificial similies based on the punning of words. Vālmīki alone describes nature with the vivacity and minuteness characteristic of English poetry. Whoever reads the description of the winter in the Araṇyakāṇḍa or of the rainy season in the Kiṣkindhā-, feels that he is himself contracting and shivering with cold or that he is dripping with rain water. We will quote one idea for each from amongst many. The poet remarks—"The thirsty elephant goes to the river to drink, but draws back his trunk at the touch of the icy water." *Svabhāvokti* is a figure of speech which Vālmīki alone uses with perfection. Again, "look at those wet clouds with their loads of water resting themselves on each top of that mountain chain." There is suppressed simile here wherein the poet compares the clouds with the labourers who are sweating under their loads and taking rest at each high place they come across.

Vālmīki is also equally powerful in conceiving and describing sublime scenes. Sublimity of conception is regarded as the peculiar characteristic of Milton and his description of the descent of Satan on earth, is often quoted as an example of his sublime conceits. Vālmīki's Sundarakāṇḍa contains some such sublime conceptions. The Sundarakāṇḍa is indeed the beautiful Kāṇḍa even from the poet's point of view. It opens with Māruti's jump across the sea which separates the Indian Peninsula from Ceylon. We must go to the original to realise what a sublime scene, the poet has evolved out of this incident, how Māruti expands his form, how he assumes the jumping attitude, how he strikes the ground and jumps up surrounded by uprooted trees flying up, how he flies through the clouds disappearing ever and anon, how his shadow runs three *yojanas* in length on the surface of the sea below terrifying the animals in that portion and making it disturbed. Further on, the palaces and apartments of Rāvaṇa are described with the sublimity of conception which characterises Vālmīki alone. Rāvaṇa is the lord of gods and demons, and it is only the unbounded imagination of a great poet which can adequately describe Rāvaṇa's wealth and splendour. But the poet rises in sublimity still further when we are introduced to Rāvaṇa's Aśoka garden and the dejected and now almost hopeless queen of Rāma. And here may be mentioned a peculiarity of Vālmīki's descriptions. It is said that Homer is fond of using what Sanskrit poets would call a *vākyopama* or a long-tailed simile as a French critic called it in ridicule. The poet raises a detailed parallel picture and thus relieves agreeably our attention. Vyāsa on the other hand is fond of using long sustained metaphors, take for instance the *śloka* भीष्मद्रोणतटा etc., where the Bhārata war is likened to a turbulent river with all its parts. Vālmīki is similarly fond of piling similes one upon another till at last the reader's mind is crushed under their load. In many of these similes the object of comparison is often an abstract noun and the similitude is very often striking even in such a case; as when the poet says, that Sītā looked like judgement clouded or hope disappointed. The description of Sītā in her forlorn and unadorned condition which the poet gives here, is splendid. This art is used by Bāṇa also in his *Kādambarī* but similes are very often artificial and strained.

Lastly, we have to consider the language. The language of Vālmīki is simple and easy. It is just such as is suited for a lyric poem, being impassioned and full of alliterative sound. It is, however, not sufficiently dignified and sonorous, nor as correct as the language of the *Mahābhārata*. But the sublime thoughts and emotions which it clothes, make you forget the inaccuracies that constantly recur. You feel as if you are borne along on the rapid stream of the Ganges inundated on some summer day by the melting of snow on the lofty tops of the Himalayas. Enchanted by the sweetest and purest water of the flood you care little for the bits of wood and chaff it carries. Such is the sublimity of Vālmīki's thoughts and such is the rapidity with which they rush into and elevate your mind.

THE RĀMĀYANA AS HISTORY

I

WEBER'S THEORY ABOUT THE STORY UNSOUND

The stirring incidents of the *Rāmāyaṇa* related in the glowing language of Vālmīki have long attracted the attention of Sanskrit scholars and thinkers, and various theories have been formulated from time to time as to their real import. Although a few see in them nothing more than the enchanting creations of a great poet, many admit and allow a substratum of truth variously interpreted. Talboys Wheeler thinks that the war between Rāma and Rāvaṇa is but a poetic version of the conflict between Brahmanism and Buddhism in the south. Nay, he goes so far as to make the suggestion that the war with the Rākṣasas may refer to the Rajput conquest of South-India in the 13th century A.D. by the founder of the Hindu Empire of Vijayanagaram. The suggestion is, however, on the face of it, absurd as the war with the Rākṣasas was exactly depicted as it is to-day, in the days of Kālidāsa who cannot be later than the 5th century A.D. and it is almost the same as we find in the last edition of the *Mahābhārata*. As already shown it cannot be later than 200 B.C. Talboys Wheeler was not a Sanskritist and hence unsound theories often find a place in his otherwise very imaginative and researchful history. Another theory is that "the *Rāmāyaṇa* exhibits the progress of Aryan plough husbandry among the mountains and forests of central and southern India and the perils of the agricultural settlers from the non-ploughing nomadic hunting tribes." By far the most formidable theory, however, is that which was advanced by Prof. Weber, who doubting that an Indian poet should have selected for his theme "an idea so abstract as the picture of the spread of Aryan civilization" holds, on the strength of the Buddhistic legend of the *Daśaratha Jātaka*, that the story of the abduction of Sītā and the war with Rāvaṇa was taken by Vālmīki from Homer, inasmuch as that story is not to be found in the Buddhistic legend. It is therefore necessary to scrutinize this theory in detail.

Mr. Telang (subsequently the Hon. Mr. Justice Telang) has already substantially refuted the theory advanced by Prof. Weber, in an excellently written brochure on the subject. But the faltering tone of the pamphlet, a tone which generally characterised Mr. Telang's utterances, leaves an impression on the mind of the reader that after all there may be some truth in the theory of Prof. Weber. That theory, however, can be more satisfactorily refuted. The whole gist of Prof. Weber's argument is to show that the *Daśaratha Jātaka* is anterior to the *Rāmāyaṇa* and that while the former does not contain the legend of Sītā's abduction, the latter which does it, was written long after the conquest of the Punjab by the Greeks which must have made the Indians acquainted with Homer's *Iliad*.

Now we have already shown in the first part that the present *Rāmāyaṇa* of Vālmīki plainly consists of an original block and substantial superstructure added at a subsequent time, like those old castles in England so vividly described by Scott in his novels. The original block can be easily distinguished from the extensive super-addition by the simplicity of its style, the archaicness of its form and its evident inconsistency with the super-structure. Prof. Weber himself admits the existence of an older *Rāmāyaṇa* though he tries to get rid of such an admission by a number of other possible suggestions. To make the subject a little clearer it may here be stated that the various versions of the *Rāmāyaṇa* may be arranged in the following chronological order—

(1) The old original *Rāmāyaṇa* of Vālmīki.

(2) The *Daśaratha Jātaka.*

(3) The Rāmopākhyāna of the *Mahābhārata.*

(4) The present version of the *Rāmāyaṇa* of Vālmīki.

For the sake of completeness may be added the later versions noticed in the first part *viz.*,

(5) The *Rāmāyaṇa* of Kālidāsa and other Sanskrit poets.

(6) The *Rāmāyaṇa* of the Purāṇas principally *Padmapurāṇa* and the *Adhyātma-Rāmāyaṇa.*

(7) The *Rāmāyaṇa* of Tulasīdāsa and other vernacular poets.

Where Prof. Weber differs from the above is, as follows. He does not clearly admit that there was an old original *Rāmāyaṇa;* at least he does not place it earlier than the story of the *Daśaratha Jātaka.*

The test of determining whether a particular version is later than another is to see whether the marvellous or mythological element is greater in the one than in the other as has been admitted by Prof. Weber himself. Applying this very test Prof. Weber has come to the conclusion that the narrative in the *Mahābhārata* is in many respects more primitive than that of the *Rāmāyaṇa* of Vālmīki. The Rāmopākhyāna in the *Mahābhārata*, therefore, is admittedly anterior to our present recension of Vālmīki's *Rāmāyaṇa.* Now this Rāmopākhyāna is on the face of it an epitome of some other work. Prof. Weber himself says, "The substantial agreement in the course of the narrative, frequently even in expression, is so very marked that we are involuntarily led to regard it as a kind of epitome of the work of Vālmīki." Nay, we may go further. Whoever reads the Rāmopākhyāna in the *Mahābhārata* is at once struck with the evident intention of the author to give an abstract of an earlier work. If then the Rāmopākhyāna is more archaic than the present *Rāmāyaṇa* of Vālmīki, and is at the same time evidently an epitome of another work closely resembling the *Rāmāyaṇa* of Vālmīki as we have it, we are driven to the conclusion that there was an older *Rāmāyaṇa* of Vālmīki which preceded the *Mahābhārata.* Prof. Weber admits as much when he says that the *Mahābhārata* contains an epitome of an earlier recension of the *Rāmāyaṇa* of Vālmīki, though he puts this as an alternative. But in our opinion it is impossible to admit any other alternative. The references to the *Rāmāyaṇa* of Vālmīki are so numerous in the *Mahābhārata* that it is impossible to hold anything else; e.g., expressions like रामायणे विविख्यातः or अपि चायं पुरा गीतः श्लोको वाल्मीकिना भुवि etc. given by Prof. Weber himself. But with the usual bias on his mind he adds "we have not succeeded in gaining here a chronological datum as we do not know when the episode *viz.* Rāmopākhyāna became a part of the *Mahābhārata.*"

It may, however, be contended that we have succeeded in gaining here a chronological datum as can be shown from what Prof. Weber himself admits elsewhere. *Rāmāyaṇa* as it exists at present was substantially in the same form before Kālidāsa wrote his *Raghuvaṁśa.* Moreover the *Rāmāyaṇa* in his days was considered as sacred as the Vedas and Vālmīki as hoary as the Ṛṣis of the Vedic *mantras.* It is very probable, therefore, as we have already shown that a long time must have elapsed between the compilation of the *Rāmāyaṇa* in its present form and Kālidāsa. In fact the date *viz.*, the beginning of the Christian era, which Prof. Weber himself assigns to the compilation after various considerations such as astronomical references, reference to Śakas and Yavanas etc., is the date which belongs to the compilation of the *Rāmāyaṇa* in its present form. Since the episode in the *Mahābhārata* is *more archaic than* the *Rāmāyaṇa* of the beginning of the Christian era, that episode must have been introduced in the *Mahābhārata* before that time. Since again that episode is evidently an epitome of a previous *Rāmāyaṇa* of Vālmīki that *Rāmāyaṇa* of Vālmīki must have existed long before the *Mahābhārata* which we now possess, and the date of which cannot be later than 200 B.C.[1]

1. Author's *The Mahābhārata : a criticism* (Delhi, 1966), p. 15.

There is not, therefore, the least doubt that there was an old *Rāmāyaṇa* of Vâlmīki which preceded the *Mahābhārata* as we have it, a proposition which Prof. Weber himself covertly admits. The chief question now is whether this old *Rāmāyaṇa* existed prior to the *Daśaratha Jātaka* or not. Prof. Weber's theory of an abstraction of the story of the *Iliad* is based upon an erroneous solution of this question. He believes *Daśaratha Jātaka* to have been the original story from which all subsequent versions have been derived. He would leave it as uncertain in how far the story of the *Jātaka* had a historical origin or whether that earliest version might also not have had as ground work, "the adventures of a demi-god, the guardian deity of agriculture hindered by exile (probably winter)." The last by the bye is making a suggestion which he himself has repudiated in another place *viz.*, the embodiment of an abstract idea like agriculture in an Indian poetic legend.

The question, however, as to whether the *Daśaratha Jātaka* contains the earliest version of Rāma's story or whether the old nucleus of the *Rāmāyaṇa* of Vālmīki which existed prior to the *Mahābhārata* was also anterior to the *Daśaratha Jātaka* is easily solved. Internal evidence convinces us that the original *Rāmāyaṇa* of Vālmīki from which the *Rāmāyaṇa* of the present day has been evolved did not represent Rāma as an Avatāra of Viṣṇu. Mr. Muir has already shown this and we have given our own arguments in further proof of it in the first part. Prof. Weber himself endorses the same conclusion in result No. 4 given at the end of his paper. But Prof. Weber does not draw out the necessary consequence of this conclusion. If the original *Rāmāyaṇa* did not contain the Vaiṣṇavite element and that element was subsequently introduced, as Prof. Weber himself says, "in the interest of Brāhmanical theology as an antidote to Buddhism" then most probably that original must have existed before the rise of Buddhism itself. Even the Rāmopākhyāna of the *Mahābhārata* contains this Vaiṣṇavite element and it is therefore probable that Buddhism must have intervened between the old *Rāmāyaṇa* of Vālmīki and its epitome the Rāmopākhyāna of the *Mahābhārata*. In short this is a cogent reason why we should believe that the original *Rāmāyaṇa* of Vālmīki was anterior to the *Daśaratha Jātaka*.

Positive arguments have been advanced by Mr. Telang to prove that the story of the *Rāmāyaṇa* was known in the days of Pāṇini and Kātyāyana, the forms Kausalyā and Kaikeyī having been explained by two Sūtras of Pāṇini. Arguments derived from internal evidence detailed in the first part also show that the old part of the *Rāmāyaṇa* discloses a state of society which existed prior to the rise of Buddhism. The worship of Vedic deities, the preponderance of sacrifice, the free eating of flesh by Brahmins and Kṣatriyas, the latter's proficiency in Vedas and Vedic rites, the greater freedom of women and their performance of Vedic rites all show a state of society, a civilization, a religion uncontaminated by feelings and ideas which had their rise in Buddhism. These arguments go a great way to prove that the old *Rāmāyaṇa* was anterior to the *Daśaratha Jātaka* which in other words is not the earliest version of the story of Rāma.

Various other considerations will also convince us that the Buddhistic legend has only adopted and in so adopting distorted a story which already existed among the orthodox Aryans of India. Let us first apply the test already noticed *viz.*, the increase or otherwise of the marvellous element to the two versions—the Buddhistic legend of the *Daśaratha Jātaka* and the old *Rāmāyaṇa* of Vālmīki—as it must have existed before the *Mahābhārata*. We find that the statement in the *Jātaka* that the shoes of Rāma struck each other whenever some injustice was done by the ministers of Bharata seems to be a silly improvement on the story of the old *Rāmāyaṇa*. But what strikes us as most ridiculous in the *Daśaratha Jātaka* is the version as to why Rāma did not return to Varanasi when Bharata offered the kingdom back to him. Be it remembered that when Rāma's step-mother asked for the boon that the kingdom should be given to her son, the king according to the *Jātaka* did not grant it as Daśaratha of the orthodox *Rāmāyaṇa* does. "The king" says the *Jātaka*, "still refusing the boon asked his children to quit the kingdom, fearing that the jealousy of the queen might procure harm to them and to RETURN *at the time of his obsequies*." He then consulted the astrologers as to the term of his life and it was declared that he would live for 12 years more. He again said to his sons "return after 12 years hence." Now unfortunately for astrology, the king died at the end of nine years and the ministers of Bharata went to call Rāma, the rightful owner back. One cannot understand why Rāma declined to return. By what obligations was he deterred from returning except by the absurd desire to follow the command of his father to the letter though he was evidently acting contrary to his real wishes—wishes not left to be gathered—but expressed *viz.*, that his sons might return at the time of his funeral obsequies ? Rāma Pandit of the Buddhistic legend is assuredly the Pandit Mūrkha of the *Pañcatantra* whose last act was to cut off and thus save the head of a friend sinking in water, in *literal* obedience to the precept—सर्वनाशे समुत्पन्ने अर्धं त्यजति पण्डितः. It speaks volumes in praise of the art or rather the truthfulness of the story of Vālmīki that Kaikeyī for whose sake Rāma had made the promise of not returning for 14 years, nowhere entreats Rāma even in the enthusiasm of the moment to return. She keeps a sullen silence possibly in the belief that in the long period of banishment in the Daṇḍakāraṇya infested by Rākṣasas harm might befall Rāma and her son would eventually be secured in the possession of the kingdom. It is possible to accept the story as told in the *Rāmāyaṇa* that Rāma in the presence of the promisee and in view of her not absolving him from the obligation, finds himself unable to return within the term prescribed. But the story of the *Jātaka* in which the king or Rāma had made no promise to the queen and in which the term was apparently prescribed by a reference to astrology but was really meant to terminate with the death of the king is evidently ridiculous and it is impossible to find any rational reason for

Rama's not returning to his kingdom when expressly asked to do so by Bharata.

The instances of marvellous additions evidently unreasonable made by the *Jātaka* may be multiplied. Lakṣmaṇa and Sītā who must have ceased to love their father with that immensity which might have existed before the long separation of nine years, are shown in the *Jātaka* to be so weak as to be supposed likely to die on the hearing of the sad news of their father's death and they were made to stand in water. They thrice became insensible when the news was broken to them and were saved by the water—a hyperbole of the most ludicrous type. The version of the *Rāmāyaṇa* is more simple and natural. The news of Daśaratha's death came upon them soon after their leaving Ayodhyā and even then they behave like mortals. They are no doubt overpowered with grief but do not make a hysterical display of it. Even Rāma laments in the most natural manner; but first deriving consolation from his own thoughts, consoles the others. There is, in short, nothing unnatural or overdrawn about the story of the *Rāmāyaṇa* which thus seems to be the original and true one.

Lastly we may notice that Sītā being represented as the sister of Rāma is a distortion not fitting in with the consistency of the story. It appears probably to have been introduced in the Buddhistic legend to create a parallel instance to the story of Buddha's ancestors having been born of a brother and sister married to each other. For it is possible to conceive that an Aryan wife was allowed to follow her husband to the jungles though in the *Rāmāyaṇa* even she is being persuaded by her mother-in-law to remain behind. But a sister would never be so allowed to go to the jungles with her brother nor had her step-mother according to the *Jātaka* any reason for wishing harm to her. If she was very young and therefore unfit to be married she would be a burden to her two brothers in their retreat to the jungles. If she was young enough to be married there was no reason whatever to allow her to be consigned to banishment for 12 years. It is impossible to see the plausibility of the story that Sītā Devī was a sister of Rāma and was allowed by her father who loved her so much, to go with her brothers to the jungles for 12 years. And it must be remembered that it is not represented in the *Jātaka* that she had become the wife of or had been betrothed to Rāma either before or during the banishment. She became his wife after Rāma's return.

Other inconsistencies might be usefully noticed. The three persons leave Varanasi accompanied by a large retinue. Now in the *Rāmāyaṇa* a retinue is expressly prohibited by Kaikeyī. But if admitting the version of the *Jātaka* there was a retinue where was the necessity of Lakṣmaṇa and Sītā saying : "we shall fetch herbs and fruits and maintain you." In the *Rāmāyaṇa* it is Rāma and Lakṣmaṇa who maintain Sītā which is more natural. The omission of all reference to flesh is also important. Then again it is said in the *Jātaka* that Daśaratha owing to grief for his sons died in the ninth year—a very short period indeed for a grieving old father to die of broken heart! And where was the necessity for so much grief? The king had himself sent away his sons to save them from the evil plan of his favourite wife. He should have been happy to know that his children were safe; and that while he did not displease his young wife and therefore himself during his life-time, he was sure that his dutiful sons would succeed him after his death. And if he felt the departure of his sons more than he had foreseen there was no oath or engagement with any person to prevent him from calling them back and arranging for their safety even in Varanasi itself. In short, these various distortions show that the story of the *Jātaka*[1] is not natural and therefore not the true one.

But these distortions were necessitated by the adaptation of the natural story of the *Rāmāyaṇa* to Buddhistic purposes. The scene as usual with Buddhistic legends, is transferred to Varanasi and the banishment or more pro-

1. See Appendix IV for the story of the *Jātaka* for purposes of comparison.

perly the retreat was to the Himalayas which was the favourite retreat of Buddhists. Why Sītā was represented as the sister of Rāma has been stated before. The retreat was for a fixed period, the term of which is settled by reference to astrology, for Buddhism was not in favour of astrology and it was intended to make a side thrust at it. The grief of Lakṣmaṇa and Sītā has been exaggerated because the story is told for the purpose of consoling a son who was grieving for his father's death. And Rāma is represented in the unnatural condition of a Buddhistic hero unmoved by grief or joy.

And here is the clue to the question why the abduction of Sītā and the war with Rāvaṇa are not to be found in the Buddhistic legend at all. One might argue in the very words of Prof. Weber himself: "The *Daśaratha Jātaka* was told for the comfort of a husbandman who was overpowered with grief for the death of his father and who left off all his avocations."[1] Now in the Rāmopākhyāna of the *Mahābhārata*, as Prof. Weber has himself observed, the sacrifice of Daśaratha and Rāma's winning Sītā by the fulfilment of Janaka's condition are not mentioned at all. Further on where Prof. Weber asks whether in the Rāmopākhyāna we may not rather have the original out of which the *Rāmāyaṇa* has been developed, he adds in a note that this could not do for the entire narrative, but from the third Kāṇḍa, Chapter XXXVI onward "as the preceding incidents in Rāma's history which were of no importance so far as the purpose was concerned for which the episode was introduced in the *Mahābhārata* (*viz.* the consolation of Yudhiṣṭhira for the rape of his wife Draupadi by Jayadratha) are accordingly entirely wanting in that poem." It is really strange that Prof. Weber can understand that the absence in the Rāmopākhyāna of the *Mahābhārata* of the details of Bālakāṇḍa does not show that these details did not form part of the original *Rāmāyaṇa* for they were not necessary for the purpose for which the Rāmopākhyāna

1. *Indian Antiquary* (1892), p. 127.

was told and yet he does not see that the abduction of Sītā and the war with Rāvaṇa were not necessary for the purpose for which the *Jātaka* was told *viz.* to console a son grieving for the death of his father, and that, therefore, the absence of these two incidents in the *Jātaka* is no argument to hold that they did not form part of the original story of Rāma. The whole theory of Prof. Weber seems to us to hang by a cobweb thread which snaps under the weight of its own arguments. There is nothing ominous or strange in the omission of Sītā's abduction and the war with Rāvaṇa in the story of the *Daśaratha Jātaka* and we may safely discard the theory of Prof. Weber as based on too slender a basis to deserve credit.

It is not necessary to discuss other theories in detail as they have been indirectly answered in what has been observed above. When it is once admitted that there was an old *Rāmāyaṇa* of Vālmīki before the rise of Buddhism which by its *Jātaka* only naturally tried to incorporate the popular heroes of the Aryans in its own theology and in its own garb, it cannot be supposed that the *Rāmāyaṇa* represents the struggle between Hinduism and Buddhism or that it represents the founding of the kingdom of Vijayanagaram. It is of course possible to contend that the old *Rāmāyaṇa* of Vālmīki which existed before the rise of Buddhism has itself no historical basis but is a mere creation of a poet's imagination. Such a theory appears all the more plausible when it is represented that the actors and the events of the *Rāmāyaṇa* are of so fabulous a character that they cannot be reduced to any consistent and natural story. We have therefore attempted in the following pages to dispel such an idea and to show that the story of the *Rāmāyaṇa* can be reduced to a consistent and reliable narrative not at all surpassing, in marvellousness, incidents which are to be found in actual uncontested history.

II

THE HISTORICAL EXPLANATION OF INDIAN MYTHOLOGY

While reading the *Rāmāyaṇa* and the history of the conquest of Mexico at about the same time we were forcibly struck with the remarkable similarity which exists between the two. The idea suddenly flashed to our mind that the ancient mythology of India might very reasonably be explained on the theory that it represents in an exaggerated form the history of the advent of the Aryans into the vast and then unknown continent of India. Working on this theory it was found that the history of the advent of the Aryans of the East coincided so wonderfully with the history of the discovery and conquest of America by the Aryans of the West that the maximum 'history repeats itself, seems to have been realised in events separated from each other by thousands of years.

The mythological history of India may conveniently be divided into three principal portions each evidenced by a separate literary work; *first*, the history of the bold adventurous Aryans of Central India typified in our gods—Indra and Viṣṇu—who, separating from their brethren the Iranians, sought new homes and found the rich regions of Afghanistan and the Punjab, Kapiśa and Gāndhāra. This history corresponds with the history of the discovery of America by the Spaniards under Columbus and the Quakers of England and France. The Vedas pre-eminently describe this period though there are some notices of it to be found in the *Rāmāyaṇa* also. *Secondly*, the history of the exploration and the conquest of the Indian continent from the Ganges southward to the southernmost point *viz.*, Ceylon, principally described in the *Rāmāyaṇa*; corresponds with the history of the conquest of Mexico and Peru glowing with the exploits of Cortez, Pizarro and other Spanish adventurers. These exploits which belong to the real history are yet as marvellous and wonderful as the deeds of fabulous knights. *Thirdly* and *lastly*, the *Mahā-*

bhārata represents and describes a great civil war analogous in many respects to the American War of Independence. The present volume is concerned with the second period *viz.*, the adventures of Rāma and other Aryan explorers as told in the *Rāmāyaṇa.* Before going on to that subject, however, we may take a brief survey of the first period in order that we may understand the second period more thoroughly. For the purposes of this survey of the first period we will try to use as far as possible the *Rāmāyaṇa* of Vālmīki itself which is the subject of our criticism in this book.

Whatever may be the explanations which European and native thinkers give about Vedic mythology in general, one fact seems admitted on all hands *viz.*, that the Devas are none but the idealised forefathers of the Aryans who came to and settled in India. They appear to have lived originally somewhere in cold and snowy regions full of the importance of fire and the sun. The Devas were a sect of dissenters from the general body of the Aryan people and had to leave their homes in consequence of their dissensions. Their favourite deity was Indra and they were fond of *soma*, that mysterious intoxicating drug which is spoken of so often in the Vedas but of which we, the present Aryans of India, have not the faintest idea. It would be beside the scope of the present work to go into a detailed proof of these propositions and we would content ourselves with giving here a few salient facts especially those that can be derived from the *Rāmāyaṇa* itself. The constant war between the Devas and the Asuras is spoken of in the Vedas as well as in the *Rāmāyaṇa.* The Devas were born of Aditi and the Asuras of Diti; and Diti and Aditi were the wives of Kaśyapa. They thus belonged to one and the same race; but as they were constantly at enmity, the word for an enemy in Vedic Sanskrit came to be *bhṛātṛvya* (भ्रातृव्य) or cousin. Again while we, the Aryans of India look upon the Devas as benevolent deities and upon the Asuras as evil ones, the Zends of Persia thought exactly otherwise. They looked upon the Devas as Devils and the

Asuras or Ahuras as angels. This clearly shows that the Zends are among the descendants of those Aryans who were at feud with the Devas, the forefathers of the Aryans of India. Indra, the favourite god of the Devas is with the Zends an infernal deity while Tvaṣṭṛ the favourite god of the Asuras is looked upon in the Vedas as an evil deity. Fire and the sun were however their common gods and are still worshipped as good deities by the Zends and the Hindus alike.

The cause of the dissensions or difference between these cousin races appears to have been the intoxicating habits of the Devas as typified in those of their favourite gods. "Indra was abhorred by the Zends as a bad power who exulted in the intoxicating *soma* and helped the wild warriors who delighted in chivalrous gallantry..." (Kunte's *Civilisation in India)*. A peculiarly interesting story in support of this idea is found in the *Rāmāyaṇa*. When from the churning of the ocean by the Devas and the Asuras, *surā* or liquor was extracted, the Asuras declined to partake of it but the Devas drank it freely. Thenceforward these two sections became distinguished by the names of *asuras* and *suras i.e.*, those who did not take liquor and those who did. What an irony on the vicissitudes of human beliefs ! Whereas in modern Hinduism, the idea of an Asura cannot be separated from bottles of liquor, in old Aryan mythology Vāruṇī was *anindita* or blameless and the Asuras were exactly those who abhorred liquor !

What *amṛta* was which came next out of the ocean is difficult to surmise. Probably it is the symbolisation of some philosophical tenet and it appears that the Devas differed from the Asuras not only in habits but also on some religious question. For these and other reasons eventually there was a secession after a great many battles between the rival factions.

Indra, the favourite deity of the Devas was probably invested with the attributes of the leaders of those Aryans who left Ariana or the ancient home of the Aryans and proceeded towards India. He conquered many a town and hence is called *purandara*. He cut roads through mountains and hills and hence is called *gotrabhid*. He incited the brave and chivalrous Aryans in their contests with the aborigines or *dāsas* and led them successfully to new lands.

दितेः पुत्रा नताराम जगृहुर्वरुणात्मजाम् ।
अदितेस्तु सुता वीर जगृहुस्तामनिंदिताम् ।
असुरास्तेन दैतेयाः सुरास्ते नादितेः सुताः । 1, 45, 37

He was hence raised to the rank of the 'king of gods'. He is the lord of the east because he led them towards the east. He is moreover also the lord of *svarga*—that happy place to the northwest of India, towards which they often looked back with affection from their new homes.

When in their further advance they came into India proper, *viz.*, the plains of the Punjab, the country was far different in climate and fertility from the lands to the north-west of India to which Indra had led them. Here they had glimmering ideas of the fair men and women who were their ancestors now idealised by them into Devas and Devakanyās. In their later settlements they were beset with new difficulties and opposed by new races. Viṣṇu, another Vedic deity appears now to have been invested with the attributes of their heroes in their new home. The position of Viṣṇu among the Vedic gods has not been discussed by Prof. Kunte in his excellent work on the history of the Aryan civilization in India. To us he appears to be pre-eminently the God of India proper, an idealisation of the last of those Aryan heroes who coming from the north-west made rapid progress in the exploration of India and the conquest of the aboriginal races. Hence he is called the youngest or the last of the gods.

यथावरेण देवानामदितिर्विष्णुना पुरा ।

His title as Upendra (उपेंद्र) can be understood when we remember that next to Indra it was he, to whom the Aryan people were indebted in the extension of their colonisation in India and the destruction of their enemies.

भ्राता भव यवीयांस्त्वं शक्रस्यासुरसूदन ।
शोकार्तानां तु देवानां साहाय्यं कर्तुमर्हसि ॥

Then again Viṣṇu is usually described in the Vedas as the long-striding god or the wide-stepping. This may as well refer to his great marches. He appears to have been the first to place his foot on the banks of that majestic river which by its volume, its rapidity, its excellent water and its great fertilising power must have struck and impressed the Aryans in their march and has, therefore, become their sacred river; and hence probably the legend that the Ganges flows from Viṣṇu's foot.

The great weapon of Viṣṇu was his bow with arrows. In fact it appears that the Aryans had by this time emerged from their primitive condition and had invented and learnt archery. Viṣṇu's bow and arrows were a great advance on the old weapons of the primeval Aryans. Indra's weapons were the *vajra* and *śakti* or a kind of javelin and Varuṇa had a *pāśa* or noose and Śiva had a *śula* or trident. Viṣṇu however had a bow with arrows and hence he became the greatest of all gods. The following quotation from the *Taittirīya Āraṇyaka* (vol. IV, Muir's *Original Sanskrit Texts)* is very significant in this connection. "Viṣṇu departed with fame; and gods followed him seeking to obtain fame. From the left hand of him a bow was produced and from the right hand arrows. Hence bow and arrows have holy origin. Though many in number they could not overcome him although he was only one. Therefore many men without bow and arrows cannot overcome one with bow and arrows." Many other quotations given by Muir show how Viṣṇu by means of his bow and arrows attained the position of the greatest of gods.

Viṣṇu thus is pre-eminently the god of India proper and historically speaking he is the idealisation of the Aryan heroes who were the last explorers of the Indian continent. In this sense we can explain the post-Vedic legends about him *viz.*, his being styled as the last of gods or Upendra, his producing the Ganges from his feet, his being described as Śārṅgī and his raising himself to the highest position amongst the Aryan gods.

These few facts about the Devas, the progenitors of the

Aryans of India and their cousins—the Asuras, about their differences and dissensions and about the two Vedic deities Indra and Viṣṇu will enable us to understand clearly the succeeding period of Aryan adventure in India as depicted in the *Rāmāyaṇa* of Vālmīki. It must be stated that this historical method of explaining Aryan deities and Aryan myths is not a new theory but is as old as the days of Yāska and others. As Mr. Tilak has pointed out in his book the *Arctic Home in the Vedas*, there always were two schools of interpretations of Vedic myths, *viz.*, that of the Nairuktas or etymologists and that of the Aitihāsikas or logographers; for instance, Vṛttra, the enemy of Indra is explained by the etymologists as a personification of Megha or cloud while the logographers say that he was an Asura and son of Tvaṣṭṛ. To us it seems extremely probable that while some of the original Vedic deities such as the sun, the wind, the dawn etc. were mere personifications of natural powers, the myths about other deities such as Indra and Viṣṇu had both natural and historical origins. While there is no doubt that they were originally personifications of natural phenomena, some myths must certainly have gathered about them based on historical events in the life of the people and it is very likely that while Vṛttra is in some myths nothing more than a cloud, in others he is the son of Tvaṣṭṛ, the god of the brother Iranians from whom the Aryans of India separated after a great struggle. It seems equally probable that still later heroes like Rāma and Kṛṣṇa[1] have some historical origin alone and it is on this basis that we have attempted to explain the apparently inexplicable story of Rāma and Rāvaṇa.

1. The character of Kṛṣṇa and of the *Mahābhārata* war as a civil war, we shall attempt to elucidate in the *Epic India*.

III

THE SUN-RACE OF AYODHYĀ

By the time the Aryans had lost all remembrance of the distant land from which they had come, they established themselves in India proper, *viz.* the Kurukshetra and the regions between the northern banks of the Ganges and the Himalayas. Their sacred rivers were now the Ganges and Sarasvatī and Kurukshetra was their holiest place. The greater part of them took to agriculture for which the country was so well fitted and for this purpose they utilised the services of some of the tame aboriginal races of the land. A common people thus formed of Aryan and non-Aryan elements soon grew up and attached themselves to the soil with that irrevocableness which has characterised the Hindu masses down to this day.

But the more intelligent and the more energetic portions of the Aryans were still actuated by that spirit of adventure which had characterised their forefathers. The Brahmins and the Kṣatriyas, soon differentiated from the *viś* or the settled people assumed that spiritual and temporal leadership of the country which naturally belongs to mental and physical energy. As between themselves difference of pursuits or division of labour had already brought about a separation, the distinction had not yet become rigid or racial. Kṣatriyas married Brahmin girls and freely gave princesses in marriage to Brahmins. Kṣatriyas like Janaka disputed the palm with Brahmins in austerities and philosophical discussion while Brahmins like Paraśurāma wielded the bow as no Kṣatriya could ever do. The Brahmins and the Kṣatriyas of the Aryan period of ancient Indian history were a noble and mighty race of men. Fair in complexion, tall in stature and powerful in frame they seemed a superior race of beings to the aboriginal inhabitants of the land. But the Aryans prided themselves more on their moral superiority and exulted in the name of *ārya* with which word they identified all that was noble, good, chaste and truthful in short, say, all that was morally sublime. The early professors of Christianity identified with great truth the name of their religion with high morality and they loved to talk of Christian piety, Christian tenderness and Christian benevolence, although much in modern times such phrases sound hollow by their empty boasts. In the same way although degenerate Hindus do not deserve the high appellation of the Aryans, their forefathers justly talked of Aryan truthfulness, Aryan chastity, Aryan benevolence and called whatever was sinful, immoral and base as un-*ārya* or not practised by the Aryans. We frequently read in the *Rāmāyaṇa* phrases like—

स्त्रीणामार्यस्वभावानां परमं दैवतं पतिः ।
यत्वमार्यं प्रभाषेथाः सत्ववान् सत्पथे स्थितः ।।

When we read उपप्लुतमिवादित्यमुक्तानृतमृषिं यथा in the *Ramāyaṇa* we are struck with admiration for the moral greatness of a people whose truthfulness must have been exemplary. Another peculiarity of the ancient Aryans of India was their intense monastic spirit. The Brahmins and the Kṣatriyas retired to the forest in the decline of life and tried to earn, by a humble and frugal life and earnest and constant devotion, the distinction of being called a Ṛṣi. This spirit was carried so far that Kṣatriyas tried to earn the distinction of a Rājarṣi by their austerities and their blameless conduct even on their thrones.

The ancient Bramins and Kṣatriyas freely ate animal food and had no objection to animal slaughter for purposes of food and sacrifice. There was no doubt some distinction between *medhya* or clean and *amedhya* or unclean animals, for Vālin says to Rāma पंच पंच नखा भक्ष्या ब्रह्मक्षत्रेण राघव. But with this exception we find little indication of any restraints as to food. The whole description as to how Rāma was regarded by his wife with different kinds of flesh, strikes us this day as rather strange and reminds us of some old powerful carnivorous German knight feasting on different kinds of animal food.

निषसाद गिरिप्रस्थे सीता मांसेन च्छंदयन् ।
इदं मेध्यमिद स्वादु निष्टप्तमिदमग्निना ।।

The principal mode of worship among the ancient Aryans was sacrifice. The ancient Aryans were in fact so mindful of sacrifice that every thing in the world; even its creation; was in their eyes a sacrifice. The Puruṣasūkta (पुरुषसूक्त) of the Vedas is a grand metaphor taken from sacrifice. Even contemplation was a sacrifice. The Brahmayajña was a sacrifice in which nothing but the Veda was to be recited. In short, sacrifice was the order of the day and in the *Rāmāyaṇa* the descriptions of hermitages of Brahmins detail how everwhere the sacrificial smoke is rising and how the sacrificial altars to various Vedic gods are arranged in their humble dwellings. The sacrifice which the bold Kṣatriya loved most was Aśvamedha. A horse was let loose followed by hosts of Kṣatriya warriors and was allowed to roam wherever he liked. Wherever he went, the Kṣatriyas claimed sovereignty for their lord. If it was denied they at once offered battle and established it at the point of arrows. In fact the Aśvamedha was a proclamation of the boundless sovereignty of the Aryans. It originated no doubt in their ambition to conquer and bring under subjection unknown regions in India; but the institution when once it had served its purpose, became afterwards a source of positive evil; for the Kṣatriyas afterwards fought among themselves for the mere pleasure of performing an Aśvamedha, the emblem of unlimited sovereignty. In the days of ancient Aryan history there was a vast scope for the ambition of the Kṣatriyas and the Brahmins. In pursuit of the idea of universal dominion, they never sat idle at home, but going abroad performed exploits which have been recorded in our national poems.

Such were the ancient Aryans of the second period of Indian mythological history. Among such Aryans reputed for their stern morality and enterprising spirit, the solar-race of Ayodhyā was the foremost. The kingdom was founded by Manu, who according to later tradition was the father of mankind and the lawgiver of the Aryan people. The genealogy of the solar-race from Manu down to Daśaratha is variously given in the Purāṇas. But certain it is that it contained many kings who were famous not only for their noble deeds but also for their intrepidity and enterprising spirit. Like the Spaniards of the 16th century, they were actuated by an enthusiastic love of the romantic. They boldly plunged into the unknown regions of India and like the Spaniards seemed to be under the peculiar protection of Providence. As in America, so in India, the work of colonisation was however reserved for another race *viz.*, the moon-race of Hastināpura.

It is difficult for men of our time, so familiar with every place in India, to conceive and to picture to themselves the feelings of the ancient Aryans who came to this vast and unknown country, then wholly or mostly under dense forests but sparsely peopled by strange races. This inability to understand their actions or to realise their feelings has contributed a great deal to invest the exploits of these bold adventurers with a haze of mystery. But fortunately for us the feelings and exploits of the Aryans of the West under similar circumstances in America, when they were brought into contact with strange countries and peoples, have been recorded in the pages of history and by their light we can rationally interpret the feelings and the doings of the ancient Aryans of India.

The first famous king of this enterprising sun-race of Ayodhyā was Sagara whose sixty thousand sons are represented to have dug the ocean in search of the missing sacrificial horse of their father. This is presumably a mythological transformation of the fact that an expedition of Kṣatriyas led by the sons of Sagara discovered the eastern ocean; and as lands and seas have often been named after their discoverers, it is probable that the ocean, of which the Aryans might not have had till then a clear idea, was named after the sons of Sagara. The expedition appears not to have taken the course of the Ganges as it was regulated by the wanderings of a sacrificial horse and hence the expedition was so fraught with perils that many perished in it. The legend goes on to relate how successive princes of Ayodhyā strove to avenge the death of Sagara's sons who were probably imprisoned and put to death by some aboriginal people with the result that the sacrificial horse never returned to Ayodhyā. Several kings appear to have made fruitless expeditions into the far east without reaching the ocean. It was reserved to Bhagīratha, the great grandson of Sagara to achieve that great purpose whereby his name has become a synonym in Indian languages for unwearied exertions in the pursuit of a fixed object. He is represented in the Gaṅgākhyāna of the *Rāmāyaṇa* to have brought down the Ganges from heaven to this earth and led her to the place where the ashes of the sixty thousand sons of Sagara lay on the coast of the ocean waiting to be purified by the holy waters of the Ganges. Thus Bhagīratha succeeded in the fulfilment of the great mission of his family. This legend has supplied Kālidāsa with a grand simile—

स सेनां महतीं कर्षन् पूर्वसागरगामिनीम् ।
बभौ हरजटाभ्रष्टां गंगामिव भगीरथः ॥

Now this legend can be reduced to a simple consistent account by a single transposition. The *Rāmāyaṇa* relates how Bhagīratha seated in a car drawn by horses, was followed by the willing Gaṅgā and how he led her in a majestic procession to the place where the ashes of his forefathers lay. Just invert the image to its natural orders as Mahomed did. "If the mountain will not come to me I will go to the mountain." And we have a consistent account as to how Bhagīratha followed the course of the Ganges and reached the sea. Probably the intelligence of the death of his forefathers must have reached Ayodhyā in that mysterious way in which tidings travel even among aboriginal peoples as we read in the history of the conquest of Mexico and hence Bhagīratha followed the course of the great river believing that it would surely lead him to the sea. Even in these days travelling on foot along the banks of the Ganges from Kanpur to Calcutta would be a great undertaking. And when that region was entirely unknown; when magnificent forests unfelled by man, rose on both sides of the vast volumes of the Gangetic water; when tigers, lions and elephants in thousands were to be seen moving about without fear of man. In fact what is now to be seen in the Sunderbunds in Bengal was much more so all along from Kanpur to Calcutta. How marvellous and difficult indeed was the exploit which Bhagīratha achieved ! Well, might this exploit in tracing the course of the Ganges be converted in popular belief afterwards into the grand legend of Bhagīratha's leading the Ganges in a great procession.

The same Gaṅgākhyāna relates how Bhagīratha performed austerities in order to bring the Ganges down from the heavens, how Śiva caught her in the meshes of his matted hair in order to humble her in her proud belief that nothing could sustain the force of her fall from heaven and how eventually Śiva was propitiated by Bhagīratha and released the sacred stream from his hair. This mythological story probably relates to the efforts of Bhagīratha to trace the course of the impetuous stream up in the high Himalayas, from whose sublime heights as from the high heaven the stream flows down. It is possible that the great forces of nature deified in the terrible Śiva, erratic and enormous as they are in the Himalayas even now, may have interposed a mountain slip in the course of the stream in the days of Bhagīratha and led to the accumulation of its water. Such a phenomenon may be conceived by what we have seen in our own days about the forming and the subsequent bursting of the Gohana lake. In Bhagīratha's days the occurrence of such a grand natural phenomenon would naturally lead to a belief that the Ganges had been caught by Śiva, the great god of the Himalayas in his hair to humble her pride and then released on being propitiated.

The exploration of the Gangetic region seems to have engaged the first kings of Ayodhyā. The later kings, the immediate ancestors of Rāma, were engaged in the exploration of the south. The name of Raghu became so famous that it soon became a patronymic of the family. What his particular exploits were, we are not told in detail in the *Rāmāyaṇa* except that he performed many sacrifices after conquering the four directions. Daśaratha, the father of Rāma appears to have penetrated far into the South. The story of his having granted two boons to his wife Kaikeyī lays the scene of his exploits in that direction. And here we come face to face with those strange people, the exaggerated representation of whose form, character and doings have been the source of various mistaken theories.

IV

THE VARIOUS ABORIGINAL RACES IN INDIA AND THEIR IDEALISATION INTO SUPER-NATURAL BEINGS

The Aryans in their march towards the south came in contact with the people of a fiercer nature and more advanced civilization than the people they had yet met with. The Vedas no doubt speak of the Yātus or Yātudhānas and of the Rakṣas (रक्ष:) called in later literature Rākṣasas but they speak more frequently of Dasyus and Dāsas as the opposers of Indra and the Aryans. These aboriginal inhabitants of the Punjab and the adjoining countries were men of a far different type from the races of the south. They were characterised more by their incorrigible thievish habits than by any higher qualities and their descendants to this day, the wandering tribes of Northern India like the Sānsis, still retain and exhibit the same character. The various races of the south on the other hand were more advanced in civilization and they either allied themselves with the invading Aryans or offered a stubborn and powerful resistance to their advance.

The names of the various aboriginal races of India may, we think, be gathered from the following couplet of *Amarakośa*—

विद्याधराप्सरोयक्षरक्षोगंधर्वकिन्नराः ।
पिशाचो गुह्यकः सिद्धो भूतोऽमी देवयोनयः ॥

The word देवयोनयः is explained by the commentator to mean देवांशकाः. *i.e.*, formed of the spirit of gods. We have already seen that the Devas were in reality the ancestors of the Aryans and were by a process of sublimation transformed into blessed angels. In the same way these races were but the aboriginal inhabitants of India subsequently sublimated into good or evil spirits according as they allied themselves with or opposed the Aryans. The word *devayonayah* therefore requires to be understood in a different sense, as we do not remember having come across any legend showing how these beings were made of the substance or rather form of gods. The explanation of this word given by *mukuta* (मुकुट) and criticised by the commentator of *Amarakośa* as ungrammatical seems to be simpler and more consistent with the traditions of the Purāṇas. He explains देवयोनयः as देवानां योनिरिव योनिरुत्पत्तिकारणमविभाव्यमिति यावत् येषाम्.[*i.e.* those whose origin like that of the Devas was unknown]. It appears probable that when the Aryans came into contact with these people they knew not their origin nor how they had come there, though they found that these races were not akin to them in origin, language or religion.

Each of these races were characterised by certain distinctive traits which have been handed down even to their descendants of the present day. The Vidyādharas were probably a race of jugglers like the jugglers of the modern day. The Apsarās and the Gandharvas were undoubtedly the ancestors of those hill-tribes still to be found on the southern slopes of the Himalayas, who are distinguished for their beauty of form and sweetness of voice and who are still characterised by marital morality of the laxest kind. The Kinnaras were an allied race with horse-like faces noted for the great love which existed between the married pair so much so that the love of a Kinnarī has constantly been taken by Sanskrit poets as the standard for comparison. The Guhyakas (गुह्यकाः) were most probably a race of gold diggers now extinct and in later literature they are supposed to be the guardians of wealth. All these including the Siddhas (सिद्धा:) are now looked upon as good spirits and their home is in the north towards the Himalayas. Probably they were all Himalayan hill-tribes and did not oppose or come into conflict with the Aryans in their advance.

The others were inhabitants of the south and were ferocious in character and odious in habits. The Bhutas (भूता:) were none but a race of timid barbarians who moved about at night and hid themselves during the day. They have been transformed into goblins and ghosts. Though now extinct in India, such primitive races are still to be met with elsewhere. The Piśācas are the forefathers of the modern Aghoris who eat the flesh of dead human beings. The loathsome practice of feeding upon the dead bodies of human beings characterises some tribes still extant in Australia and America and it is no wonder that there might have been some races in India too in bygone days. In later mythology the Piśācas were believed to be the ghosts who frequent the burial grounds and feed upon human corpses.[1] Still more dreadful were the Rākṣasas who fed on living as well as on dead human beings. They now appear to us as creations of the imagination but their reality can be admitted from what we read of the ferocious yet civilized Aztecs of Mexico. As connected specially with the history of Rāma's adventures we will treat of them separately along with the kindred race of the Yakṣas.

There were other races still who inhabited ancient India and whose names are not mentioned in the above couplet, races distinguished by names of animals. They came subsequently in popular belief to be looked upon as

One is here reminded of a story in the *Kathāsaritsāgara* in which a Brahmin boy shivering with cold went near a burning corpse for warmth when a streak of fat suddenly bursting from the burning body entered his mouth and he was immediately transformed into a Piśāca. It is impossible to believe that a streak of fat getting into his mouth by accident should have had such a miraculous effect as to invest him immediately with superhuman power for evil.

being in form and character the animals themselves whose names they bore. But it is easy to recognise in the serpents, the monkeys, and the bears such human races that bore these names either owing to some fancied resemblance in face to these animals or owing to having worshipped them. These beings also were gradually invested with superhuman powers and were classed in the days when the present edition of the *Rāmāyaṇa* was compiled with Yakṣas and other supernatural beings. Whenever any great event occurs these supernatural beings are said to appear in the sky to witness the grand sight and often shower flowers from their position of vantage. So we read in the *Rāmāyaṇa* when Paraśurāma was defeated by Rāma,

> गंधर्वाप्सरसश्चैव सिद्धचारणकिन्नराः ।
> यक्षराक्षसनागाश्च तद्द्रष्टुं महदद्भुतम् ॥

That the Rākṣasas, the future enemies of Rāma should so far have forgotten themselves as to collect with the other blessed beings in the sky, clearly shows that things had so far changed even in the days of the last compiler of the *Rāmāyaṇa;* that the Rākṣasas were looked upon as entirely different beings from what they actually were. A very long time indeed must have elapsed between the real events and the modern compilation of the *Rāmāyaṇa*, an interval which had so transformed the Rākṣasas that their original and true character was entirely hidden under the haze of supernatural powers subsequently attributed to them. We shall endeavour in the next few pages to divest them of this supernatural haze and exhibit them in their true delineations showing at the same time how exaggerated notions must have gathered about them in course of time.

V

THE RĀKṢASAS, THEIR ORIGIN AND THEIR ABODE

The Rākṣasas have been confounded in later mythology with the Asuras and we must at the outset correct this confusion of ideas. While the Asuras were brother Aryans most probably the forefathers of the Zends of Persia, the Rākṣasas were an entirely different people being the aborigines of India. The Asuras, as Indian mythology itself represents, were the sons of Diti, the co-wife of Aditi and inhabited the same country as the Devas. They performed the same sacrifices and worshipped the same gods. The story of Yayāti marrying the daughter of the Asura king Vṛṣaparvan when he had strayed away from his own kingdom into that of the Asura king, shows in what close proximity the Indian Aryans and the Asuras once lived and the relations they bore towards each other. In short the Vedas and the early Aryan mythology support the now generally accepted theory that the Asuras were brother Aryans. Even in the *Amarakośa* the names of the Asuras are given immediately after those of the Suras or gods.

The Rākṣasas on the other hand were an entirely different people and their names are given in the *Amarakośa* after those of Yama. Their origin is thus described in the *Rāmāyaṇa.* "Brahmā having created the waters, created beings for their protection. Some of them who were hungry, cried 'we will protect'; others who were not hungry cried 'we will sacrifice.' The first Brahma named Rākṣasas and the second Yakṣas."

रक्षाम इति तत्रान्यैर्यक्षाम इति चापरैः ।
भुंक्षिताभुंक्षितैरुक्तस्ततस्तानाह भूतकृत् ॥१॥
रक्षाम इति यैरुक्तं राक्षसास्ते भवंतु वः ।
यक्षाम इति यैरुक्तं यक्षा एव भवन्तु वः ॥२॥

The above is an instance from among many of the curious ways in which Sanskrit poets and Purāṇa writers often seek to explain names by some fancied similarity of sound. We may, however, safely draw two inferences from the above story *viz.*, that the Rākṣasas were a race of men who lived on the sea-coast and protected the waters and that unlike the Yakṣas, a kindred race. They were characterised by great voracity, in other words, that they were ferocious cannibals. That the Yakṣas and the Rākṣasas were kindred races will appear also from the fact that the name पुण्यजन was borne by both and the same fact is also apparent from the relationship which Kubera, the king of the Yakṣas, is said to have borne to Rāvaṇa; and in this sense we can understand the legend that Laṅkā originally belonged to Kubera who subsequently vacated it in favour of his brother Rāvaṇa. The two races probably lived originally in the south of India from which the Yakṣas were gradually ousted and driven towards the north by their ferocious brethren.

To return to the latter it will have sufficiently appeared from the story in the *Rāmāyaṇa* related above that the Rākṣasas were a cannibal race living on the southern sea-coast of India. Traces of this race of cannibals are still to be found in the Andamans, in Borneo, in Sunda and other islands of the Indian ocean. At the time the Aryans invaded southern India, a race of Rākṣasas named Salaṅkatāṭaṅka is mentioned in the *Rāmāyaṇa* as living in Laṅkā. It is probable that the genealogy of Rāvaṇa by which on the father's side he is connected with the Aryan Kaśyapa is a spurious representation of later days. On the mother's side Rāvaṇa is even in the present *Rāmāyaṇa* represented as having been born of the race of Salaṅkatāṭaṅka, a name which has undoubtedly an aboriginal sound about it. It reminds one of the name Xicotencatl borne by one of the chiefs of Tlascala in the history of the conquest of Mexico. We may believe that a race of cannibals distinguished by that name occupied Ceylon in the days of Agastya.

Whether the Rākṣasas originally lived in this island and thence extended their settlements and conquests into India or whether they inhabited India originally, it does not seem clear. But there is no doubt that they held sway like the Mexicans over a vast expanse of territory beyond the limits of their small kingdom. They had many outposts under their commanders at different places as far as Janasthāna and Rākṣasas were even to be found as far north as the southern bank of the Yamunā river itself. The Ṛṣis in their complaints to Rāma said, 'the Rākṣasas kill persons living near Pampa and even along the bank of the Mandākinī and on Citrakūṭa mountain.' Viśvāmitra's sacrifice was performed on the southern bank of the Ganges and for this sacrifice he had to seek the aid of Rāma against threatened interruptions by Rākṣasas. It appears thus probable that the Rākṣasas inhabited the Indian continent far towards the north upto the Jumna river and the southern bank of the Ganges and the Jumna combined.[1]

The name Yamunā or 'sister of Yama' was probably given to this intervening river by the Aryans on this very account. In their advance from the Punjab towards the south they found little obstacle till they crossed this river. In Rāma's days the Aryan settlements extended along the northern bank of the Ganges and there were a few between the Ganges and the Jumna. Whenever the Aryans crossed the Jumna they were attacked and the unfortunate carried away by the terrible Rākṣasas whose cannibalism must have impressed their minds vividly. The Jumna thus probably earned an unenviable notoriety and was consequently appropriately named the sister of Yama.

The name 'Nairṛtas' again given to Rākṣasas and that of Nairṛtya given to the south-western direction may be explained on the same basis. *Nirṛti* means hell and the Rākṣasas might well have been called the sons of hell. The Aryans who had established themselves on the north of the Ganges as far as Bihar, extended their settlements through western Bengal towards the south and south-west and here they came into contact with the Rākṣasas whom they called नैर्ऋता: or the sons of hell. The south western direction was accordingly also named नैर्ऋत्या, the abode of Nairṛtas. The southern direction too might have been appropriated to Yama for the self-same reason showing how disastrous were the attempts of the Aryans to

1. Even the Vedas speak of the Yātudhānas or Rākṣasas as the eaters of men and the disturbers of sacrifices. Indra and Agni are constantly invoked against them who, therefore, seem to have carried their excursions even beyond the Ganges.

penetrate and colonise the south. These various facts and the fact that Daṇḍakāraṇya extended southwards from the Yamunā itself as appears from Rāma's first taking his abode on Citrakūṭa in fulfilment of his promise to reside in the Daṇḍakāraṇya for 14 years, show that the Rākṣasas inhabited though sparsely, that portion of India which extends to the south of the Yamunā and that their chief kingdom was in Laṅkā or modern Ceylon.

VI

THEIR PERSONAL APPEARANCE AND THEIR CANNIBALISM

The modern idea of a Rākṣasa is so terrible and absurd that it is necessary to describe their personal appearance in detail to show that the modern idea has no basis whatsoever in the old *Rāmāyaṇa* of Vālmīki. The Rākṣasas were no doubt dark in complexion like most of the modern inhabitants of southern India. The *Rāmāyaṇa* abounds in descriptions in which the darkness of their colour is brought into relief by the side of the fair complexion of the Aryans. Fair Sītā, as she is carried away by black Rāvaṇas, is beautifully compared to a golden girdle encircling a dark elephant—

सा हेमवर्णा नीलांग मैथिली राक्षसाधिपम् ।
शुशुभे कांचनी कांची नीलं गजमिवाश्रिता ॥

Again नीलांजनचयोपम: and similar other epithets are usually used in connection with the Rākṣasas and would not be far amiss if applied to many a Dravidian of the present day.

But though dark in colour, the Rākṣasas were not ugly in appearance. They had regular features which often were striking and handsome. Such examples of pleasing countenances are frequently to be met with even in these days among the dark inhabitants of southern India. The *Rāmāyaṇa* constantly represents many Rākṣasī women as comely and beautiful. रूपयौवनसंपन्ना रावणस्य वरस्त्रियः. Māruti saw both comely and ugly men and women in his nocturnal progress through Laṅkā—विरूपान् बहुरूपांश्च सुरूपांश्च सुवर्चसः. Even Rāvaṇa is described by Māruti as handsome—वृतमाभरणैर्दिव्यैः सरूपम् कामरूपिणम्. Māruti saw these Rākṣasas when asleep and hence it cannot be suggested that they had assumed an adventitious form, considering the belief which always prevailed that the Rākṣasas assumed their own real form when asleep or after death.

Now these descriptions are inconsistent with the modern idea of a Rākṣasa, a terrible being with dishevelled hair, protruding tongue, eyes like red balls, teeth jutting out like those of a tiger, an awfully forward chin and huge arms while a Rākṣasī as popularly conceived, would be too hideous to describe here in detail. Probably the Rākṣasas have been invested in later days with these terrible forms because they were the enemies of mankind. Amongst all people mythological dragons and fiends have always been assigned hideous and unnatural forms but the old *Rāmāyaṇa* of Vālmīki does not support such a conception of the Rākṣasas who were then believed to be ordinary mortals. An interesting passage in support of this, is to be found in the Yuddhakāṇḍa wherein Rāma asks the monkeys never to assume the form of a man so that there would be seven men only on their side including Vibhīṣaṇa and his followers and that they could thus safely kill whoever might be in human form except those seven.

न चैवं मानुषं रूपं कार्यं हरिभिराहवे ।
वयं तु मानुषेणैव सप्त योत्स्यामहे परान् ।।
अहमेव सह भ्रात्रा लक्ष्मणेन महौजसा ।
आत्मना पंचमश्चायं सखा मम विभीषणः ।।

The commentator adds एवं च अस्मान् सप्त हित्वा मनुष्याकारो निःशंकं वध्यः वानराकारो वानरैर्युध्यते तदा वध्य एव. That the Rākṣasas had *ordinarily* human forms, was thus conceded even in the days of the last editor of the *Rāmāyaṇa*.

The general belief about the hideousness of the Rākṣasas might have originated in another way. When Sītā was kept in confinement by Rāvaṇa, she was surrounded by a number of ugly women of the most distressing deformities with a view to terrify her. The possibility of Rāvaṇa's having such women in service is strengthened by what we read of the collection of human deformities made by Montezuma, the proto-type of Rāvaṇa. "I must not omit" says Prescott "to notice a strange collection of human monsters and dwarfs and other unfortunate persons in whose organisation nature had capriciously deviated from her regular laws. Such hideous anomalies were regarded by the Aztecs as a suitable appendage of State." It is possible that Rāvaṇa too had such ugly and uncouth deformities of nature in his service. The impression which a number of such deformed beings constantly surrounding her, must have left on poor Sītā's mind, might have led subsequently to an exaggerated notion about the hideous persons of Rākṣasas and Rākṣasīs.[1]

The Rākṣasas were probably a strong race of men physically, tall in stature and big in dimensions, like some of the Kamathis of southern India of modern days, and Kumbhakarṇa was probably the biggest of them.

यस्य प्रमाणाद्विपुलं प्रमाणं नेह विद्यते

only means "a bigger man than whom was never seen." This is intelligible and we must regard as a mere exaggeration, the modern idea of Kumbhakarṇa *viz.*, that he was as tall and big as a mountain and that ten thousand Rākṣasas and elephants had to walk over his body to wake him up. This number itself shows that the generality of the Rākṣasas was not as big as is usually supposed. They were only ordinary human beings. All such exaggerations may safely be rejected as the conceptions of later poets who tried largely to use hyperbole for the purpose of poetical embellishment.

The cannibalism of the Rākṣasas again must have contributed to increase or even to originate the popular distorted idea about their form. It would have been difficult to imagine a whole nation much advanced in civilization

1. The ten heads of Rāvaṇa and his twenty arms will be explained later on.

and yet addicted to the detestable practice of feeding upon human flesh, had it not been for the instance afforded by history so late as the 16th century, in the Aztecs of Mexico. The Rākṣasas like the Aztecs fed and feasted on the flesh of living human beings. Probably they ate the flesh of men of their own race and did not always depend for human flesh of captives from other people and hence they were called Yātus as well as Yātudhānas. The *Rāmāyaṇa* no doubt describes the Rākṣasas as eating other kinds of flesh also *viz.*, of beasts and birds and even eating vegetable food. But the Rākṣasas exulted in cannibalism and were always in high glee whenever they met with an enemy and had an opportunity of satisfying their unnatural craving.

This horrible practice of preying on one's own race, rare as it is, even among the brute creations of God, no doubt once obtained among some human races—Aryan and non-Aryan, Western and Eastern. But the most favoured and forward races of the world soon gave up the horrid practice and advancing in civilization and power, they destroyed and stamped out the races who still practised it. In the words of Prescott, it was beneficently ordained by Providence that the land of the Rākṣasas should be delivered "from the brutish superstitions and practices that festered there." And like Cortez, Rāma was, if nothing more, a deliverer of humanity, a hero who by a chain of events which we shall presently go on to relate, was under the wise dispensation of the Almighty, brought into conflict with the detestable Rākṣasas and who eventually purified the land from the debasing practice of cannibalism. For the Rākṣasas who were, as might have been expected from their food and physique, a race of fierce men inplacable in their hatred and unfeeling in their conduct, waged an unceasing war with their enemies and like the terrible man-eaters of the jungles knew no medium between death and dominion. The Rākṣasas of Laṅkā like the Aztecs of Mexico thus fought with the Aryans and their allies to the bitter end and were eventually almost annihilated.

Such were the Rākṣasas in reality, a strong powerful race of men, black in complexion, fond of red garments, ferocious as well as cunning and given to the dread habit of cannibalism but after all human beings only who subsequently in Aryan mythology were transformed into evil-minded voracious supernatural beings who were constantly at feud with the Aryans and who always interfered with their sacrifices and other Vedic rites.

VII

THEIR EARLY CONFLICTS WITH THE ARYANS

It is natural to expect that the Rākṣasas, before Rāma led his army against Laṅkā, had several conflicts with the Aryans who were slowly extending their conquests and settlements into southern India. The Rākṣasas, as has been already stated, used to overrun the country as far north as the southern banks of the Ganges and the Yamunā. It appears that the Aryans first came into conflict with the Rākṣasas in western Bengal where the Aryans had extended their settlements from across the Ganges to the north of which they had in Vedic times already founded the kingdom of Videha or Bihar. For the *Rāmāyaṇa* lays the scene of Vāmana's conquest of Vālin in this part of the country; at least Vāmana is said to have performed austerities here on the southern bank of the Ganges in order that he might succeed in conquering Vālin. Vālin is no doubt represented as an Asura, but very probably he was a Rākṣasa as an Asura had no business to be in the south of the Ganges. Though the *Rāmāyaṇa* generally treats the Rākṣasas as distinct from the Asuras, it often confounds the two. Vālin's wife is called Vindhyavālin, a name which suggests the idea that he reigned among the Vindhya mountains which extended as far as the southern bank of the Ganges near Mirzapur. It is also possible that Vālin's being driven to Pātāla, represents that the Rākṣasas were eventually pushed back to the south of that range.

Viśvāmitra's Siddhāśrama was situated on the southern bank of the Ganges and is described by him to be situated in the same place where Vāmana performed his austerities. The Aryans appear thus to have entered the south from the north-east through Orissa and by the eastern coast. But this way was too circuitous and unhealthy. It was therefore extremely desirable to cross the mountain regions of the Vindhya range which offered for some time a great and unsolvable difficulty. The credit of overcoming it was reserved for Agastya who was undoubtedly the pioneer of the Aryan settlement in the south proper. He penetrated deep into the country, crossed the Vindhya and cognate hills and established a colony on the northern bank of the Godāvarī near Janasthāna which seems to be well identified with the flat rich country of the modern Maharashtra. Like Viśvāmitra, he was both a warrior and a priest and himself fought with the Rākṣasas and almost freed the intervening territory from their pest. In fact, the south was explored and colonised by him and hence this direction has well been appropriated to him in Hindu mythology. A star in the heavens conspicuous for its brightness and situate in the southern hemisphere has been named after him in the same way as the seven stars of the Great Bear in the north and named after the seven great Ṛṣis of Vedic times.

The following *ślokas* from the *Rāmāyaṇa* will bear out and support the above observations.

निगृह्य तरसा मृत्युं लोकानां हितकाम्यया ।
दक्षिणा दिक् कृता येन शरण्या पुण्यकर्मणा ॥
तस्येदमाश्रमपदं प्रभावाद्यस्य राक्षसैः ।
दिगियं दक्षिणा त्रासाद्दृश्यते नोपभुज्यते ॥
नाम्ना चेयं भगवतो दक्षिणा दिक् प्रदक्षिणा ।
प्रथिता त्रिषु लोकेषु दुर्धर्षा क्रूरकर्मभिः ॥

The legend hinted at in the next *śloka*

मार्गं निरोद्धुं सततं भास्करस्याचलोत्तमः ।
संदेशं पालयंस्तस्य विन्ध्यशैलो न वर्धते ॥

and given in detail in another place is as follows : The great Vindhya range grew so tall and high that it threatened to stop the very progress of the sun. Agastya on being supplicated by the Ṛṣis promised to stop the growth of the presumptuous mountain and thus to prevent the happening of such a calamity. He presented himself before the range when the mountain in reverence fell prostrate before him. Agastya asked him to remain in that position till he returned. But he did not return and the mountain still lies prostrate awaiting the return of the great sage. This myth may easily be rationalised thus : The range together with the allied Satpura range is very broad and the mountainous region extends almost from the southern bank of the Ganges through Central India and the Central Provinces to the Berars which may be said to form the northern part of the Deccan. In ancient times it was extremely difficult to cross this mountainous region and it was Agastya who boldly crossed these ranges and permanently settled in the Deccan never returning to Hindustan. He thus showed the crossing of the Vindhya practically possible or metaphorically speaking the Vindhya range has lain low forever ever since it fell prostrate before Agastya. Many sages or Brahmins followed Agastya and in Rāma's time there were many Āśramas or settlements of Brahmins in the Deccan to the north of the Godāvarī.

Vāmana, Viśvāmitra, Agastya and other settlers were all Brahmins[1] but they had constantly to bend the bow in defence of their settlements and cultivations against

[1] Probably Kṣatriyas did not accompany the Brahmins in their settlements in the south; a fact which is borne out by the extreme paucity of the Kṣatriya population to be found to the south of the Vindhya range even at present. In northern India, the Kṣatriyas form a preponderating portion of the population and can be identified even now as Aryans. In the south however very few real Kṣatriyas are to be found except the Marathas and the Vadyaras and a few other mixed races. Even the Pāṇḍyas of ancient India were a mixed race as appears probable from the prevalence among them of incestuous marriages.

the ever troublesome Rākṣasas who frequently raided them from their strongholds in further south. Agastya's prowess as a warrior and his exploits against the Rākṣasas have already been noticed. And we gather the same thing from the fact that he is represented to have given to Rāma, a bow, a sword and a set of quivers.

इदं दिव्यं महच्चापं हेमवज्रविभूषितम् ।
वैष्णवं पुरुषव्याघ्र निर्मितं विश्वकर्मणा ॥
अमोघः सूर्यसंकाशः ब्रह्मदत्तः शरोत्तमः ।
दत्तो मम महेंद्रेण तूणी चाक्षय्यसायकौ ॥
महाराजतकोशोयमसिर्हेमविभूषितः ।
जयाय प्रतिगृह्णीष्व वज्रं वज्रधरो यथा ॥

Here, we have a historical sequence. The mantle of Indra and Viṣṇu as the fighters of Asuras and Rākṣasas, the enemies of the Aryans, fell upon Agastya and Agastya transferred it to Rāma.

The Central Provinces or the Daṇḍakas were still a dreaded tract and the Brahmin settlers though warriors, had, in their engrossing intellectual, religious or agricultural pursuits, often to invoke the assistance of the Kṣatriya kings of northern India. The sage Agastya told Rāma that Daśaratha was his friend and we even find that Daśaratha is said in the *Rāmāyaṇa* to have led several expeditions to the Daṇḍakas against the Rākṣasas. In one of these expeditions he is said to have given a boon to his wife Kaikeyī for having saved his life. The Daṇḍakas or the mountainous regions between the Ganges and the Godāvarī were thus, in spite of scattered Brahmin settlements, assisted by the Kṣatriya kings of the north, a dreaded country and served the same purpose as Siberia does to Russia in these days as a place for exiled princes to be sent to, to fight with the Rākṣasas or die. It was in fact the scene of many conflicts between the Aryans and the Rākṣasas before the time of Rāma who, however, was unquestionably the greatest hero who fought against them. His exploits, marvellous and almost imaginary as they at first sight appear to be, have a solid substratum of truth which may well be understood in the light of what we read about the incredible adventures of Cortez in Mexico. And Rāma was a hero of a still higher order than Cortez. His war with Rāvaṇa was not provoked by him nor did he play that unfeeling part which Cortez did towards the Mexicans. Above all, his pure and sublime life stands unequalled and without a rival. It is this as well as his marvellous exploits which have raised him to divine honour in India and we will now go on to sketch that noble life from such historical light as can be gathered even from the hyperbolical account of the *Rāmāyaṇa* as it at present is.

VIII

RĀMA'S BIRTH, EARLY LIFE AND MARRIAGE WITH SĪTĀ

Daśaratha, the aged monarch of Ayodhyā had three consecrated queens but no son. An Aryan of the truest Vedic type, he pined for progeny and his anxiety increased as old age grew upon him. In this extremity he was advised by his preceptor Vasiṣṭha to perform an Aśvamedha. In the eye of the Vedic Brahmin, an Aśvamedha could give anything that was desired—sons, riches, heaven and even absolution. A sacrificial horse, the emblem of unlimited sovereignty was accordingly let loose by orders of the aged king. There was nobody to dispute the sovereignty of the great sun-race of Ayodhyā and the horse duly returned or was brought back to the sacrificial ground at the end of one year. Meanwhile for the whole year Daśaratha and his three queens had performed very many sacrifices and religious ceremonies under the guidance of Vasiṣṭha assisted by many sages. The horse on its return was killed by the heroic Kausalyā, the eldest queen, with three strokes of a sword and the various parts of the animal's body were duly burnt as oblations in the sacrificial fire. The sacrificial session concluded with great rejoicings and with feasts and liberal presents to learned Brahmins.[1]

In due course, the three queens of Daśaratha conceived and gave birth to four sons. We may here attempt to explain the efficacy of the Aśvamedha sacrifice in giving sons to the aged monarch on a natural basis. Princes and princesses and rich men and women in their luxurious and pampered habits are denied the blessings of progeny unless they practise continence for a long time at intervals; and sacrifices and vows are ordained by the Hindu religion for the purpose of securing such abstinence as well as of providing holy occupation to their minds which would otherwise run riot with evil thoughts. It is not to be wondered, therefore, if a religious vow, a sacrifice or a long pilgrimage which ensures abstinence, purity of mind and also emaciation of the body is often prescribed with success to princes and rich men and women for the purposes of securing progeny.[2] Whatever may be the true explanation,

1. The story of Ṛṣyaśṛṅga and his performing here after a *putreṣṭi* or son-giving sacrifice is evidently an interpolation. The contradictions and repetitions involved in this interpolation have been noticed elsewhere.

2. We may here notice two strange theories which have been built upon the fact that Rāma himself had no children till his return to Ayodhyā after the conquest of Laṅkā. Weber thinks that the fact goes to support the Buddhistic legend that Sītā was the sister of Rāma and as such lived in the forest marrying him only after his return to Ayodhyā. Under such a view one may be disposed to doubt whether Daśaratha had been at all married to Kausalyā and his other two queens until he performed the Aśvamedha. Moreover, we have already shown that if Sītā had been the sister of Rāma she would not have been consigned to the forest along with Rāma nor is it probable that a Kṣatriya lived unmarried for 14 years with a sister whom he was at liberty to marry. The whole theory of Weber is so flimsy that it requires no further refutation. Talboys Wheeler makes the still more absurd suggestion that Sītā had conceived of Rāvaṇa who might have subjected her by force to live with him and that Rāma abandoned her again on account of this suspicion. Now Rāma could well have marked if Sītā was pregnant at the time of her deliverance from captivity.

the three queens of Daśaratha gave birth to four sons of great beauty and promise. Rāma the son of Kausalyā was the eldest, the brightest and the strongest of all. Next to him was Bharata, the son of Kaikeyī the youngest and the most beautiful wife of the old monarch and Lakṣmaṇa and Śatrughna were the sons of Sumitrā, his intermediate queen. The four boys in due time grew into four handsome, powerful Kṣatriya princes. Rāma was the most powerful of all as might have been anticipated from his strong and heroic mother. They were instructed in archery as well as in the Vedas as all Kṣatriyas of Vedic times were. A Vedic Kṣatriya was like his German brother both a warrior and a priest although his duty called him more frequently to arms than to the alter. The patriarchal form of family government was then the predominant form and the father was the master of the family in the most unmistakable manner. The same position was occupied by the eldest brother in the family and Rāma was loved and respected just as a father by his three younger brothers though he was especially served by Lakṣmaṇa. Bharata, the son of the favourite queen, was similarly served by Śatrughna, but inspite of his jealous and imperious mother, Bharata was not behind his other brothers in his love and respect for Rāma. A touching picture is drawn in the *Rāmāyaṇa* in one *śloka* of how in patriarchal times a younger brother loved and served his elder brother.

यदा हि हयमारूढो मृगयां याति राघव: ।
अथैनं पृष्ठतोऽभ्येति सधनु: परिपालयन् ।।

[As Rāma riding a horse went a-hunting, his brother

Nay, he could have made himself sure on the point by watching the time of her delivery, if there was any doubt on the point. It is strange that such wild theories should find a place in the work of such a great historian as Talboys Wheeler. We, for our part, think for reasons noted in the text that it does not at all seem surprising that the union of such a loving pair as Rāma and Sītā after a painful and anxious separation for one year should be followed by the birth of not one but two sons.

Lakṣmaṇa used to follow him on foot bearing his bow].[1]

One day after the boys had finished their education in the Vedas and in archery, the sage Viśvāmitra came to Daśaratha's court all of a sudden. He was duly hailed and worshipped by the old king and asked his mission. To his great concern and amazement Viśvāmitra asked him to lend him the services of Rāma to protect a sacrifice which he was going to perform against the molestations of the Rākṣasas. The aged monarch who loved Rāma as dearly as his own life prevaricated. He knew the perils of a fight with the treacherous Rākṣasas and would go himself with his army to watch over the sacrifice. But the sage declined this offer; in fact he would take none but Rāma as perhaps he had other things in his mind besides the sacrifice. At last Daśaratha was compelled to grant the request of the venerable Ṛṣi, and Rāma followed by his beloved brother Lakṣmaṇa set out with the great sage for his hermitage.

They crossed many small rivers and then the great Ganges at its confluence with the Sarayū, the river of Ayodhyā. On their way, the sage regaled and encouraged the princes by relating stories about their ancestors' exploits especially those of Bhagīratha who had traced out the whole course of the Ganges. The young princes were probably fired with an ambition to equal if not surpass their great ancestors by their own future achievements.

As soon as they crossed the Ganges, they came into regions exposed to the raids of hostile aboriginal tribes. That particular region was infested by Yakṣas, a weak race cognate to the Rākṣasas. Tāṭakā, a Yakṣa woman hailed the advent of Rāma with a shower of stones and was killed

1. Vālmīki's account of Rāma's childhood and education is so simple, brief and decorous that it is impossible to believe that Talboys Wheeler had access to the original fountain of the *Rāmāyaṇa* when he gives long extracts from other works containing puerile matter on this period of Rāma's life. See Wheeler's History Vol. II, pp. 29-34.

by an arrow from his bow. They then pursued their way unmolested to Siddhāśrama, the hermitage of Viśvāmitra. Here everything was ready. The sage immediately entered on the performance of his long projected sacrifice while Rāma and Lakṣmaṇa kept an unremitting watch. For five days no interference was attempted but on the sixth a number of Rākṣasas appeared and Rāma was ready to receive them. He killed their leader Subāhu with an arrow when his brother Mārīca with the other Rākṣasas fled away to the Vindhya mountains. Viśvāmitra was highly pleased with the courage of the boy warriors, and being himself a great master in the art in days by-gone taught them many useful lessons in archery.

Hearing of a sacrifice being performed at the house of Janaka, Viśvāmitra thereafter set out for Mithilā, Janaka's capital, accompanied by the two princes. He knew of Sītā, the marriageable daughter of Janaka, and also of his vow to give her to him who would bend a heavy old bow. Viśvāmitra was convinced of the prodigious strength of Rāma, his young pupil and desired to secure Sītā for him. The Ṛṣi together with the princes once more crossed the Ganges and reached the confines of the great city of Janaka.

Here comes in the beautiful story of frail Ahalyā. She was the wife of Gautama, the preceptor of Janaka. In a weak moment she had consented to co-habit with Indra but had been discovered by Gautama. The enraged husband not only cursed Indra but also cursed his own wife and condemned her to live a life of separation and perform a dire penance. It appears probable that when Rāma and Viśvāmitra came, the sage Gautama, remembering that she had been sufficiently punished, forgave her and allowed her to do the duties of hospitality to his distingusihed guests. Such is the original story of the *Rāmāyaṇa* of Vālmīki over which later mythology, later than even the *Rāmāyaṇa* of to-day, has spun a beautiful web *viz.*, that Ahalyā was cursed to become a stone and in that condition she lay there for ages until she was remetamorphosed by the purifying touch of Rāma's foot-dust.

After partaking of the hospitality of the reunited pair; the party went into Janaka's town. Janaka came out to receive the venerable sage and was highly impressed with the appearance of the Kṣatriya princes who accompanied him. There was no *svayamvara* then at Janaka's house, no assembling of kings including Rāvaṇa himself, as modern mythology represents, ready to try their hand at the bow for the beauteous bride. Janaka asked Viśvāmitra who the princes were and Viśvāmitra acquainted him with their names and object. Thereupon at Janaka's command a large heavy box was brought out by a number of men and opened. Rāma easily took the bow out of it and strung it, in doing which the old wood suddenly gave way and snapped with a fearful sound.[1] Janaka was overjoyed at the fulfilment of his almost impossible vow by so young and desirable a bridegroom and having finished the sacrifice immediately ordered preparations for the marriage. Daśaratha was informed in Ayodhyā of the marvellous feat of strength performed by Rāma and was invited to celebrate the auspicious ceremony of Rāma's marriage. The bridegroom's party duly came to Mithilā and on the appointed day Vasiṣṭha and Śatānanda, the son of Gautama, began the ceremony by reciting the great lineages of Rāma and Sītā respectively in true Rajput fashion. The sage Viśvāmitra opportunely suggested that the union of such illustrious families should further be cemented by the marriage of the three younger brothers of Rāma with the three daughters of Kuśadhvaja, the brother of Janaka. The happy suggestion was joyfully accepted by both and the old kings and the old Ṛṣis enjoyed the happy function of the marriages of their children and pupils.

We may here incidentally notice the question how Sītā

[1] It is said to be the bow of Śiva deposited with the family. There is however no attempt here to bring out the antagonism between Śaivism and Vaiṣṇavism for neither existed in the days of Vālmīki or Janaka. The poet simply wishes to mark the greatness of the bow when he says that it belonged to Śiva. At another place it is said to be the bow of Varuṇa.

came to be looked upon as *ayonija* or not human born. Probably the original *Rāmāyaṇa* of Vālmīki did not represent her as such. For in the very first *sarga* which, as we have already shown, appears to be very old, she is said to have been born in Janaka's family. The commentator sees the contradiction evidently involved herein and tries to gloss over it. The later idea that Sītā was born of a furrow of the earth, seems to have originated in a too literal interpretation of the name, as the word *sītā* also means a furrow and popular belief which in later times identified her with Lakṣmī, was fain to imitate the *Mahābhārata* which represented Draupadī as having been born of the sacrificial fire. The *Rāmāyaṇa* in another place represents accordingly that Sītā was found by Janaka as he was ploughing a field himself, which is in itself an improbability.[1] A similar tendency to interpret names too literally has been the source of a far more absurd belief as we shall have to show later on.

Having celebrated the marriages, the old king Daśaratha with the four married couples joyfully returned to Ayodhyā, the only event on their march home being a meeting with Paraśurāma, the reputed enemy of the Kṣatriya race, an incident which, whether historical or allegorical, has very little connection with the story of the *Rāmāyaṇa* and is not necessary for the march of its events.

IX

THE SLIP BETWEEN THE CUP AND THE LIP

Twelve years elapsed since the marriage of Rāma with Sītā. Rāma was a man of sufficiently mature age and experience. His father thinking himself now too feeble to carry on the administration resolved to appoint him as *yuvarāja* or Crown Prince. A council of state consisting

1. तस्य लांगलहस्तस्य कृषत: क्षेत्रमंडलम् ।
अहं किलोत्थिता भित्वा जगतीं नृपते: सुता ॥

of priests, citizens and feudatories was called and consulted. The council was unbounded in its praise of Rāma and approved of the resolution of the king most unhesitatingly. Preparations for the ceremony were thereupon immediately ordered and it was proclaimed that Rāma would be consecrated *yuvarāja* on the day following.

The city immediately put on its gayest appearance. Flags were raised, streets were watered and scented with incense, houses and palaces were decorated and illumined, temples were strewn with flowers and the people turned out in their gaudiest apparel. Probably this description of the scene in the *Rāmāyaṇa* is taken from what the last editor actually saw of a great city like Pāṭaliputra under a great prince like Agnimitra, for, as we shall show elsewhere, temples had no existence in the days of Rāma and there was not that grandeur of public demonstration in his sturdy days. But we may take it that the city with such means as the civilization then existing afforded, did its utmost to celebrate the great occasion.

Everybody was pleased to see the happy and joyful appearance of the city—everybody, except the envious nurse of Kaikeyī, the young and beautiful wife of Daśaratha. As she looked on the city from the top of the palace, she felt that her own importance as the *dhātrī* or nurse of the favourite queen was fading in the proposed elevation of Rāma and necessarily therefore of Kausalyā, his mother whom she might have affronted on many an occasion. She, therefore, set to work on the captious mind of her wayward mistress. She informed her that her husband was about to appoint Rāma as *yuvarāja* taking advantage of Bharata's absence at his uncle's house and represented that she had thus been affronted and levelled to the dust; that Daśaratha only flattered her and called her his dearest while in reality he favoured Kausalyā and Rāma. She soon succeeded in poisoning her mind against the proposed elevation of Rāma and advised her to ask the two *varas* or boons granted to her by Daśaratha long ago. Now was the time for their fulfilment; by one Bharata might be appointed *yuvarāja*, by the other Rāma might be banished to the Daṇḍaka forests where the Rākṣasas, the dreaded cannibals, as she well knew, frequently raided the Aryans and ate them up. The capricious queen was soon convinced of the necessity of taking this step and resolved to get it done.

The aged unsuspecting monarch came as usual to pass the night with the favourite queen and found her much infuriated. With hair dishevelled she lay in a bed of ashes and would hear of nothing until he had promised her what she would ask for. Daśaratha would give her anything and the heartless queen repeated what she had been taught. The monarch was laid prostrate at the astounding demand for Rāma's banishment. He entreated her again and again and in every possible way tried to desist her, but Kaikeyī was not to be moved from her purpose and the morning made the monarch pale, breathless and bedridden. Ministers and priests assembled at the palace at the appointed time ready to take part in the joyous ceremonies of investiture when lo ! the king was reported to be ill and unable to move. At the command of the imperious queen aquiesced in by a nod from Daśaratha, Rāma was sent for. Sītā who had been fasting and praying the whole previous night fondly bade him god-speed, hoping to see him return decorated with the insignia of Royalty. She did not suspect that God had ordained it other wise.

Rāma appeared before the monarch and was thunderstruck to find him ill, grieving and speechless. He entreated him to speak kindly to him as usual but the throat of the monarch was choked. He asked his step-mother the reason of Daśaratha's miserable condition and the artful woman told him that Daśaratha had promised her to appoint her son as *yuvarāja* and to banish Rāma to the Daṇḍakas for fourteen years and that he would not speak until Rāma had departed. The king uttered a cry of abhorrence and tears broke forth from his eyes. Rāma now comprehended the situation and tried to assuage his father. He told Kaikeyī that he was quite ready to leave the kingdom to Bharata and go into exile and that he would rather see his father redeem his promise and avoid disgrace than that he (Rāma) should enjoy the royal dignity for which he had no particular love. The crafty woman was fain to catch him at his own word and bade him prepare and leave the kingdom that very day.

Rāma, sad at heart, yet trying to conceal his emotions, went to inform his mother Kausalyā of the sudden change in his destiny. It was a death blow to her high hopes. Even with Rāma, the pet of his father, she was held as of no account; but without him she would be insulted at every step by her imperious co-wife. She was consoled by Rāma and told that it was both her and his duty to obey his father's wishes. At last she acquiesced and said she expected nothing less from her son born of Daśaratha. She would wait and suffer for fourteen years at the end of which period she implored him not to fail to return and bless her old age.

Historians have made much of the suggestion made at this interview by fiery Lakṣmaṇa that the old dotard who forsook his eldest son for the sake of his favourite queen should be imprisoned and Rāma should take possession of his rightful patrimony. The *Rāmāyaṇa* represents that even Kausalyā approved of this suggestion.[1] These dishonourable thoughts of the two were undoubtedly momentary and have been brought in by the poet most probably to show how sometimes wicked thoughts flit across the minds of the most honourable persons, when one's fondest hopes are suddenly blasted by misfortune. Fiery Lakṣmaṇa, who could not brook to see his eldest and rightful brother suddenly deprived of his birth-right or the aged queen goaded by jealousy and about to lose the support of her son, might have had the criminal idea

1. Talboys Wheeler suggests on the strength of this approval that Daśaratha might have been poisoned by Kausalyā when the former after Rāma's departure took refuge at her palace and died of a broken heart.

for a short time. Such momentary feelings were however soon overcome and both the brother and the mother of Rāma consented to his going into exile in odedience to his father's boons.

Rāma went thence to his own house where his fond wife every moment waited to see him return with all the pomp and dignity of a would-be king. But her heart failed within her as darting forward she saw Rāma return devoid of dignity and dejected in appearance; and she fervently asked "wherefore this ?" The poet touches an exquisite chord of human nature when he represents the patience of Rāma by which he had supported himself so long, suddenly forsaking him as he saw his dear loving wife, the partner of his joy and glory, grief and disgrace before him. It would have been unnatural had he still shown Rāma, as in the Buddhistic legend, calm and without feeling. It would have been overdrawing the picture of frail humanity. Rāma with evident anguish and tearful voice explained to his wife the altered nature of his fortunes and bade her prepare for a long, long separation from him during which time, with bitterness of feeling, he enjoined her to lead a meritorious life and obey without grumbling the orders of Bharata who would be the king-elect.

But the loving wife was not thus to be shoved off. She insisted on her accompanying him to the jungles. A wife was the only partner of her husband's joy and misery. With Rāma, jungles were as pleasant to her as heavens; without him even palaces were as tormenting as hell. Rāma was strong enough to protect her, otherwise with Kṣatriya pride she observed he was not a fit son-in-law of Janaka. She would never complain or murmur or give him trouble. She would please him by her company, nay, she would walk in front of him crushing the very thorns with her feet and thus making the path smooth and easy for her dear husband. Nothing is more touching and full of imagination. Vālmīki's art is here sublime. She made light of all the difficulties of a life in the jungles and implored her husband with tears bathing his broad chest and her heaving bosom not to leave her behind but to take her with him. Rāma thus assured of her constancy and courage at last told her that he had simply put her to the test and that without her heaven itself was to him quite tasteless. He asked her to prepare at once to go with him, distributing all her things amongst her friends, servants and Brahmins.

Lakṣmaṇa, the faithful follower of Rāma now came forward and begged to be allowed to accompany them. Rāma tried in vain to dissuade him and at last he too was allowed to go. Riches and other possessions which the three had, were then distributed amongst servants, friends and Brahmins and the three started from their home barefooted for the palace to take leave of their beloved father. What a strange vicissitude in their fortune ! Instead of a Crown Prince riding in a golden chariot and fore, with elephants preceding and horsemen following the crowded people in the streets saw Rāma, a begger walking on foot followed by his faithful wife and brother on foot. As the truth gradually came to their knowledge they cried "shame on Kaikeyī, shame on the old dotard. Poor Rāma and Sītā are being cheated by the wily woman of their rights." But Rāma and Sītā and Lakṣmaṇa silently pursued their course and arrived at the palace. Daśaratha was at once informed by the chamberlain that Rāma, Lakṣmaṇa and Sītā wishing to take leave of him awaited at the gate.

The old monarch with a view to allow all his wives to have a last look on the courageous young prince called together all his wives. Three hundred and fifty fair women with blood-red eyes followed the fainting Kausalyā to the royal presence and Rāma was asked to enter. The loving father ran forward to embrace his darling child but fell senseless from remorse and exhaustion. He was raised by his weeping children and again placed on the couch. When he came to his senses, Rāma entreated him to allow his son to depart with a calm and easy mind and to allow Lakṣmaṇa and Sītā who would not stay behind to go with him; for he was the lord and master of all his children. The desperate monarch in his frantic effort to prevent his son from going away said : "Thy father, Rāma, has been duped by Kaikeyī into giving her two boons. Imprison him and rule thou in his stead." But Rāma was too good a son to take that course even with his father's consent. He told his father that he was by right and experience the proper person to rule the earth and that for himself he did not love a kingdom at all. Daśaratha thereupon ordered his minister to send with Rāma servants and stores and treasures that would make his life in the jungles easy and comfortable. But the scheming Kaikeyī was alarmed and world not hear of it. "My son Bharata would not accept an empty kingdom" she exclaimed "any more than one would take the dregs in a beer pot from which another has drunk the beer." Daśaratha cried "shame, shame" but the shameless woman stood unmoved. At last Rāma interposed and said that such royal comforts did not suit the life of an ascetic which he was bound to lead and that hermits wanted only garments of bark and spades to dig. Kaikeyī at once had these brought and placed before the three. Rāma without any ado put on the bark garment and Lakṣmaṇa followed suit. But fair Sītā who knew only how to put on silk garments was frightened on seeing two garments of Kuśā grass placed before her and with tears in her eyes and the garments in her hand she looked at her husband, as handsome as a Gandharva prince, and said in confusion "how do the wives of ascetics put on garments of grass ?" There she stood aimlessly handling the garments about her neck abashed and confused and looking as if she would swoon every moment. The sight of the weeping princess never used to such indignities drew tears from the eyes of the ladies of the palace and in their anguish with one voice they cried "Rāma, do not take Sītā with you; she has not been banished, blessed Sītā is not fit to live in the jungles like a hermit." But Rāma did not mind their words and running to the rescue of his simple wife tied the garment about her neck over her own silken sari.

Such is one of the most beautiful and touching picture

imagined and depicted by Vālmīki, the greatest of Sanskrit poets. The scene is so pathetic and at the same time beautiful that we realise in it the very essence of tragic poetry, the feeling of pleasure and pain overpowering us simultaneously. Even Vasiṣṭha was roused to see the woeful plight of the high born princess, the daughter of Janaka and the daughter-in-law of Daśaratha, and reviling the woman-fiend Kaikeyī, he threatened to follow Rāma to the jungles and leave the city a jungle for her son. Daśaratha too cried "what sin has poor Sītā committed ? What has she done to you that you give her garments of grass" and he ordered silken saris and ornaments to be given to her such as she would require in her exile.

The chariot was ready which was ordered to take Rāma to the confines of the kingdom of Kosala. And Rāma feeling that it was necessary to cut short the interview to leave without delay, made his last bow to his father, then to his mother and then to the rest and hurried out of the palace. The parting words of Sumitrā to her son Lakṣmaṇa, as he made his last bow to her, were beautifully pithy. "Look upon Rāma as Daśaratha, upon Sītā as myself, thy mother, and upon the forest as the city of Ayodhyā and go, my son, without any fear."

Rāma got into the chariot followed by Lakṣmaṇa and Sītā and the charioteer Sumanta put the lash to the horses. A cry of woe suddenly burst forth from the palace and Daśaratha coming out ran after the chariot calling upon Rāma to stay, to stop a while. But Rāma did not hear or appeared not to hear till at last the chariot got out of the sight of the feeble monarch and he fell senseless in the streets of Ayodhyā.

When he came to his senses he asked to be taken to the apartments of Kausalyā where the aged pair passed six days and nights in wailings and lamentations when at last on the seventh, the broken-hearted Daśaratha expired crying "Rāma, Rāma, beloved of thy father, where hast thou gone ?" In the hour of death, the remembrance came upon him of once having shot an arrow at a supposed elephant drinking at a pond on a summer night and killed by accident a young man who was filling his pot with water for his thirsty blind aged parents. Daśaratha was touched to the quick on hearing a human cry and descending saw the dying young man. According to his instructions he took the pot to his blind-parents who however would not take it of him, recognising that it was a stranger and not their darling son. They at last threw themselves on the dead body of their child and expired cursing Daśaratha that he too would die wailing like them for his son. Such is the story of Śravaṇa's death and his parents' curse which was too literally fulfilled, a story which is as pathetic as ever was conceived (if untrue) by a poet.

We have given the account of Rāma's exile from Ayodhyā and Daśaratha's death, at rather great length in order to acquaint the reader with the poetical merits of the Ayodhyākāṇḍa, the finest part of the *Rāmāyaṇa*, so simple and devoid of exaggeration yet so pathetic and morally sublime. As the descriptions and dialogues proceed, the reader weeps and weeps and feels that the thing is actually happening before his eyes. The moral effect of the whole is also so powerful that it will forever remain a noble and divine example before the Aryans of India, inciting great men to keep their promise at any cost, good sons to obey their parents, noble wives to cheerfully share the lot, however miserable, of their husbands and misguided and obstinate women not to pursue too far lest they earn the title of a veritable Kaikeyī. Without exaggeration and without absurdities, by means of a simple truthful story[1] the poet so rouses our feelings and rivets the lessons of ordinary life so strongly upon our minds that they sink deep into our hearts and we feel strong and courageous in the performance of our duty under any circumstances.

1. It is strange that the above incidents are contemptuously dismissed by a short sentence in Hunter's big History of India. "A *zenana* intrigue resulted in the banishment of Rāma to the Daṇḍakāraṇya.

X

THE FAITHFULNESS OF BHARATA

Pending the choice of a successor, the dead body of Daśaratha was immersed in an oil cistern in order that it might not decompose, a curious procedure which is not to be found in later Aryan history. A Council of State was convened and the question as to a successor was discussed. It was resolved at the suggestion of Vasiṣṭha that Bharata should be called back from his grandfather's and should reign in accordance with the wishes of his father. Messengers were accordingly despatched to bring him immediately. They were asked to make no mention of Daśaratha's death or Rāma's exile. Perhaps Vasiṣṭha was afraid that Kaikeyī's father and brother might themselves seize the kingdom for reasons which will appear hereafter. The messengers reached Girivraja, the capital of the king of horses as he is called, and informed Bharata that he was badly wanted in Ayodhyā, discreetly observing in reply to his query "They were indeed blessed and happy about whose welfare he so anxiously inquired." Bharata immediately took leave of his grandfather and uncle who gave him valuable presents and started back for Ayodhyā.

The minute description of the way taken by the messengers on their way from, and the route taken by Bharata on his way to, Ayodhyā is important so far as ancient geography is concerned and will be noticed in a subsequent volume. But we cannot proceed without noticing here the fact that Bharata's grandfather lived at a great distance from Ayodhyā probably in modern Afghanistan or still further west. The word Kekaya has a Persian sound and reminds one of Kai Khousru or Kaikobad. The fact that he was called Aśvapati still further strengthens the inference as Persia has all along been noted for its beautiful horses. The nature of the presents given to Bharata also corroborates the same view. They included variegated blankets or shawls and deer-skins, as well as dogs reared in the harem with large bodies and powerful jaws and swift and well trained asses. The mention of powerful dogs and well trained asses jars upon the ears of the modern Hindus accustomed as they are, to look upon these animals as unclean. That the king of a country between Persia and Afghanistan should give his daughter in marriage to a king of Ayodhyā shows that in the days of Rāma, the Aryans of India still kept social relations with their brother Aryans beyond the Indus whose fair daughters it was the usual custom with Indian kings to espouse and who were probably not much differentiated from them by habits, feelings and religion.

Another circumstance in connection with the Aśvapati is of great importance in the same connection. It is stated in the Ayodhyākāṇḍa (chapter CVI) that king Daśaratha when he married Kaikeyī, gave his whole kingdom to the Aśvapati as *śulka* or bride's price. The custom of taking money from the bridegroom prevailed, it appears, amongst the Aryans beyond the northwest frontier. And it is curious to note that the same custom was pleaded by Mādrī's father when he gave her in marriage to Pāṇḍu, and Bhīṣma had to give large presents to the Mādra king in return for his daughter. The Persian or the Iranian Aryans who were the cousins of the Aryans of India have already been identified with the Asuras of Indian mythology and the fact that this kind of marriage is called *asura* in the Smṛtis shows that the Aśvapati was an Asura or Iranian Aryan. We shall have to refer to this subject later on.

To return to Bhārata, he reached Ayodhyā with great haste but was surprised to find it cheerless. He passed through the city with a heavy heart and entering the palace saw and saluted his mother. She was delighted to see him return safely—him for whom she had done so much, told him all that had happened thinking that he would be pleased and called upon him to wear the hard-won crown. But Bharata was too good a son and too faithful a brother to enjoy a kingdom so wickedly obtained. He wept bitterly for his father who had died with a broken heart and for his brother who had been exiled for no fault of his own. He reviled Kaikeyī for her cruelty and swore that he would call back Rāma from the forest if for nothing else, but to disappoint her in her cruel ambition. At the instance of Vasiṣṭha, the usual obsequies to Daśaratha were performed by the disconsolate Bharata whose tears did not cease during the twelve days of mourning. He refused the crown offered by the State Council and said he would go himself to bring back Rāma from the forest. Orders were accordingly given for preparations to march immediately.

After the pioneers had prepared a way in the jungles, Bharata set out with a large army, accompanied by the family priest and his three mothers. He arrived soon at Śṛṅgaverapura which Talboys Wheeler (perhaps wrongly) places on the other side of the Ganges. The town was ruled by Guha, a Niśāda king and a friend of the rulers of Ayodhyā. By means of boats supplied by Guha, the army crossed the Ganges into the Doab then a perfect jungle and marched towards the confluence of the Ganges and the Yamunā where Bharadvāja had established an Āśrama or Brahmanic settlement consisting of persons who generally led a religious life but who were agriculturists and warriors also when occasion required.

Bharadvāja duly received Bharata and Vasiṣṭha and disected the former to the Citrakūṭa hill on the other side of the Yamunā where he himself had asked Rāma previously to take up his residence. It is strange that there is no mention of the manner in which Bharata's army crossed the Yamunā though we have a graphic description of how Rāma crossed the deep stream before. There was no boat or ferry there as the whole of the region to the south of the river was uninhabited. Rāma and Lakṣmaṇa made a float of dry rafters of wood bound together with rope-like creepers. The chivalrous and powerful princes then placed Sītā on the float and swam with it across the river. The description of the feat reminds one of the adventures of those hair-brained Spaniards who floated down the unknown Amazon for miles on a float of rafters similarly constructed.

Having crossed the river with great difficulty Rāma had built a hut on an eminence of the Citrakūṭa hill, where also dwelt some leaders of Brahmin colonists of the Daṇḍakāraṇya. There Rāma sat in front of his hut, amusing Sītā with bits of various kinds of flesh, clad in the fashion of devotees in garments of bark and with matted hair. There Bharata found the very image of beauty, strength and high resolve in him. Bharata overcome with grief fell at his feet and Rāma raised him up and embraced him like his own child. Rāma learnt from him the sad news of his father's death, and visibly affected said to his companions "Sītā, thy father-in-law is dead and Lakṣmaṇa, thy father. Bharata tells me the fearful news that the king of Ayodhyā has gone to heaven." The three then went down to a river near by and having bathed offered water and oblations to the departed monarch. On their way back they met with Kausalyā, Sumitrā and Kaikeyī, the sage Vasiṣṭha and others. The meeting between the mother and the son, the priest and the pupil, the people and their rightful prince was at once painful and happy.

When the first out-pourings were over, Bharata requested Rāma to return to Ayodhyā and accept his rightful crown. Rāma, however, firmly declined and averred that he had promised his father at the request of Kaikeyī to reside in the Daṇḍakāraṇya for fourteen years and he was bound to keep his promise. However much Bharata reviled his mother and offered the kingdom again and again, Rāma was immovable.

At this juncture Jabali adopting the language of an atheist said "Who is your father and what do you owe to him ? These relations are mere accidents. Why do you not enjoy the kingdom offered to you by Bharata of his own accord ? Why do you think of things which are merely inferential and reject what is certain and visible. *Śrāddhas* and sacrifices have been invented merely to induce people to make gifts. If oblations given in *śrāddha* can reach the deceased or his soul in another body, why not oblations and offerings made to an absent friend reach him and satisfy his hunger ?"

Such are some of the stock arguments advanced by atheists in later times (Jains and Buddhists included) against the orthodox ritual, which probably the last editor has amplified in order to afford him an opportunity to refute them by the mouth of Rāma. The dialogue is the only one in the *Rāmāyaṇa* wherein we find philosophical questions discussed and atheistic and Buddhistic dogmas refuted. Some of the observations of Rāma in reply are full of eternal and universal truth and of abiding moral interest. His praise of truthfulness is indeed sublime and he told Jabali that truth was dearer to him than every thing else especially because :—

> E'en as the king is, so his subjects are;
> A kingdom rests on truth and righteousness.

Vasiṣṭha then tried orthodox arguments based on the rule of primogenitive observed in the family but he too failed to induce Rāma to return and Bharata at last said "If I rule in Ayodhyā I will do so in your name and would burn myself on a pyre if you did not return at the end of fourteen years." He then requested Rāma to place his feet on two sandal pieces ornamented with gold which he will take with him to Ayodhyā as a token of his viceroyalty. He did not enter the city but stopped outside at a villa named Nandigrāma where he took up his residence and from whence he ruled the kingdom in the name of Rāma's golden sandals.

Rāma too feeling his presence at Citrakūṭa very near Ayodhyā and fearing a repetition of visits by his afflicted brother and mother, left Citrakūṭa and plunged deeper into Daṇḍakāraṇya. He first came to the Āśrama of Atri and his benign and affectionate wife Anasūyā. He thereafter visited several settlements of Brahmins who everywhere hailed his advent to the Daṇḍakāraṇya as a great boon for they were frequently harassed by the incursions of cannibals or Rākṣasas who had their strongholds in the south. They showed him the dead bodies of the Aryans killed by the dread cannibals in much the same way as the Spaniards found human beings sacrificed in various temples in their march through the Mexican country. Rāma passed several years among these settlements and had frequent encounters with the Rākṣasas. At last by the advice of Agastya who had penetrated the forest farthest, Rāma established himself on the Godāvarī which was the very frontier of the Rākṣasa kingdom—Janasthāna or modern Maharashtra.

XI

THE ABDUCTION OF SĪTĀ

The interesting incidents recorded in the preceding pages are taken from the Bāla and Ayodhyākāṇḍas of the *Rāmāyaṇa* and have nothing supernatural or extra-ordinary about them. The events on the other hand which are recorded in the Araṇya and succeeding Kāṇḍas are apparently so wonderful, so highly improbable, and so miraculous that they are usually treated as imaginary or fabulous. How could there be a golden deer or how could a Rākṣasa, even if he is a cannibal, have ten heads and twenty arms? How could monkeys speak and combining with men fight with the Rākṣasas ? How could a monkey leap across a strait which is at least a hundred miles in breadth or two human beings only with the assistance of monkeys overcome every obstacle and destroy a whole nation of cannibals ? Such are, among others, some of the most wonderful absurdities related in these Kāṇḍas which must be explained before we can reduce the subsequent narrative to something like an historical account.

But if we scan the *Rāmāyaṇa* even as it exists at present carefully, we shall find that many of those absurdities did not belong to the original poem of Vālmīki or are such as proceed from the naturally exaggerated impressions of a people penetrating for the first time into an unknown country covered with unfelled forests and coming into contact with strange races of men. When these later interpolations or natural exaggerations are removed by the light of what is recorded to us of the historical conquest of Mexico by the Spaniards placed under similar circumstances, we shall have left behind a sufficiently intelligible and probably historical chain of events as we shall now proceed to show.

Some of the greatest events in history have only an humble beginning. And curiously enough the history of the conquest of Laṅkā begins like the history of the conquest of Mexico with the love of an aboriginal woman. Śūrpaṇakhā said to be a sister of Rāvaṇa, the king of Laṅkā, lived in Janasthāna with whose people Rāma and Lakṣmaṇa must have had some intercourse from their hermitage on the Godāvarī. She fell in love with the pleasing countenance of Rāma and in a straightforward manner offered to marry him. Rāma who had already a far better wife declined the offer and suggested, perhaps in jest, perhaps in half earnestness, that she should take Lakṣmaṇa to husband.[1] The woman was not displeased with Lakṣmaṇa's face which was not much worse than that of Rāma but Lakṣmaṇa too declined to accept her either because he did not like her appearance or because he thought that his marriage would interfere with his duty to his elder brother. He, therefore, returned the joke observing that Rāma should abandon his ugly wife and take instead a far better partner in life. Śūrpaṇakhā's vanity was flattered and with the fearful love of a Rākṣasī she said that she would at once devour Rāma's ugly wife and ever afterwards live with him happily without a rival. She was not content with mere words but at once moved with a menacing attitude to attack poor Sītā. Amazed Rāma interposed and catching hold of her, handed her over to Lakṣmaṇa and asked him to condignly punish her. Lakṣmaṇa cut her nose off with sword disfiguring perhaps an already ugly woman for her dastardly attack on Sītā.

The wailing woman went to her relatives in Janasthāna,

1. Instances of Spaniards marrying Mexican wives are to be found in the history of the conquest of Mexico.

loudly demanding vengeance on the unceremonious strangers. And a number of Rākṣasas with Khara and Dūṣaṇa at their head at once came out with the object of destroying the two persons who had dared to insult the Rākṣasa kingdom. Rāma and Lakṣmaṇa had already guessed what was going to follow and reaching Sītā to a place of safety had taken a position of vantage from whence they could take good aim at the attacking enemy as also defend themselves easily against them. A battle ensued in which the Rákṣasas were defeated, both their leaders being killed and the survivors fleeing away in terror. This amazing victory of Rāma was the beginning of his great renown and the fear in which he was held thereafter by the Rākṣasas and is frequently referred to in the *Rāmāyaṇa* with pride.

चतुर्दशसहस्राणि रक्षसां भीमकर्मणाम् ।
हतान्येकेन रामेण खरश्च सहदूषण ॥

[Fourteen thousand Rākṣasas of dread deeds were killed by the single Rāma and so was Khara with Dūṣaṇa]. Probably the number of his opponents is exaggerated but there is no reason to doubt the truth of his great victory. The historian of the Mexican conquest tells us that at the battle of Ottumba, less than 200 Spaniards with no other weapons except sword and lance defeated an opposing force of sturdy, obstinate Mexicans variously estimated at one to two hundred thousand. Prescott thus moralises on the incredible battle of Ottumba, which was the beginning of the conquest of Mexico. "It is almost as difficult to form an accurate calculation of the numbers of a disordely savage multitude as of the pebbles on the beach or the scattered leaves in autumn. Yet it was undoubtedly one of the memorable victories achieved in the new world. And this, not only on account of the disparity in the forces but of their unequal condition. For the Indians were in all their strength while the Christians were wasted by disease famine and long protracted sufferings, without cannon or fire arms which had so often struck terror, deficient even in the terror of a victorious name. But they had discipline, desperate resolve and implicit confidence in their commander." And further, the Rākṣasas though individually strong like the Aztecs formed an unwieldy mass which could not make profit out of its numbers. Rāma and Lakṣmaṇa were on the other hand conversant with the tactics of a fight. Like the Spaniards they first brought down the commanders of the enemy's army which when deprived of its guiding spirits was helpless like a ship deprived of its rudder. But the chief secret of Rāma's victory, to our mind, lies in his possession, and his great mastery in the use of the bow and the arrow. It appears probable that the Rākṣasas and the aboriginal races of the south did not know the use of a bow. They fought with sticks and stones and the only missile they used was a *śakti* or javelin. The monkeys who were an equally powerful race but who were not cannibals used the same weapons *viz.*, sticks and stones and this fact together with their uncouth appearance and shrill yells might also have secured to them that name. The bow and the arrow was thus to these aboriginal races a dreadful weapon and struck the same terror among them as the fire arms of the Spaniards did among the Aztecs. By means of the bow, the Aryans could shoot down their enemies from a very long distance while they themselves stood at a place where the javelins or the stones of the enemies could not reach. It was, therefore, that one man with the bow as the *Aitareya Brāhmaṇa* (already quoted) has put it "could not be conquered by many." The ancient Aryans of India developed archery to a remarkable degree and Aryan heroes attained proficiency in it by constant practice which, as we shall have occasion to show elsewhere, struck even the Greeks with admiration. We need not, therefore, wonder at the success of Rāma and Lakṣmaṇa when they defeated and routed an army of several hundred barbarians in Janasthāna.

Śūrpaṇakhā thus completely discomfited yet thirsting for revenge went now to the court of Rāvaṇa, the great king of the Rākṣasas in further south. There she found him seated in council, endowed with a powerful body, gorgeously bedecked with jewels, though dark in colour and stern in appearance yet possessing a handsome countenance, the master of a thousand beautiful wives all brought together by force. In order to cover her own fault she cunningly distorted the truth and told Rāvaṇa that she wanted to seize, for his sake, the wife of Rāma, the most beautiful woman she had ever seen, when Rāma prevented her and had her nose cut off. Fourteen thousand Rākṣasas went to avenge her insult but were routed by Rāma and Lakṣmaṇa with great slaughter and Khara and Dūṣaṇa were slain. Rāvaṇa, indeed, was lying idle and apathetic when he allowed such indignities to be inflicted on his own kith and kin and the power of the Rākṣasas. The barbarian king was struck with the description of Sītā's beauty much more than with the insult offered to his great name and with the instinct natural to a Rākṣasa he at once resolved to abduct Sītā while he laid an ambuscade to kill her husband and his brother.

Rāvaṇa started on his evil errand accompanied by his friend Mārīca. The subsequent events have been so beautifully conceived and described in the *Rāmāyaṇa* that they form another scene in the poem which is poetically sublime. As Rāma, Lakṣmaṇa and Sītā sat in front of their hut, Mārīca appeared before them in the disguise of a golden deer with jewelled eyes. Sītā, a woman after all, took a fancy to the deer and requested Rāma to bring it alive. Rāma ran after it in order to fulfil his love's wish. A little after, a cry was heard as that of Rāma and Sītā believing that he was in danger, asked Lakṣmaṇa to go to his rescue. He told her that Rāma was unassailable by any body and that it was merely a *māyā* or deception practised by the wily Rākṣasas. But she upbraided him for his unconcern and even went the length of expressing her suspicion that he had an evil eye upon her and therefore wished Rāma dead. Stung to the quick Lakṣmaṇa left her confiding her with the greatest reluctance to the care of the mute trees and the hermitage.

After a few minutes came a gentle devotee, a fine reddish garment thrown on his naked well formed body and a stick and a wooden pot slung over his left shoulder. He seemed struck at finding a beautiful woman in a lonely place and asked her who she was and how she came there. Sītā hospitably received him, told her history succinctly and finally requested him to wait till her husband returned *with a load of deer flesh.* The devotee now explained to her that he was Rāvaṇa, the lord of Rākṣasas and the master of untold riches. He told her that he was smitten with love for her and would make her his principal queen and requested her to leave the dispossessed and poor Rāma to his fate and accompany him to Laṅkā where she might rule and enjoy a mighty kingdom. Indignant and amazed Sītā told him plainly that in comparison to Rāma he looked like a jackal before a lion, a veritable mouse, and that he would lose his life if he did not desist from his base design. Rāvaṇa's rage was now roused and striking the palm of his left hand with that of his right, he suddenly assumed a terrific form as big as a mountain with ten heads and twenty arms. Even the trees of the jungle seemed to shake in fear and the Godāvarī shrank within herself and ceased to run. Seizing the frantic woman he walked towards his chariot. A great vulture named Jaṭāyu who sat on an emience, saw his dastardly act and flew at him and killed his horses. But he was not a match for Rāvaṇa who after a short struggle threw him down and cut his wings. Taking Sītā again he flew into the sky and shortly reaching Laṅkā placed her in confinement in a garden called Aśokavana under the guard of uncouth Rākṣasī women.

Such is the poetical and marvellous story of Sītā's abduction which a little reflection will show as somewhat unnatural. It looks indeed unnatural that Sītā should have spoken to Lakṣmaṇa those harsh words, or should have unsuspectingly told disguised Rāvaṇa every thing about herself forgetting what Lakṣmaṇa had just said about the *māyā* or deceit of Rākṣasas. And if she was so guileless and simple, how did she not tell Rāvaṇa that she had seen a golden deer, that Rāma had gone to catch it, that she had heard an anxious cry from him and that he, Rāvaṇa too, should go to his assistance. The fact that she merely says that Rāma will soon come back with *a load of the flesh* of different kinds of animals killed, shows as we have elsewhere noticed, that the story of the golden deer is a later addition. It appears that Rāma and Lakṣmaṇa had both gone out on a hunting expedition as usual confiding Sītā to the care of Jaṭāyu an aboriginal servant and that Rāvaṇa abducted her after slaying Jaṭāyu, while he had told off Mārīca to lie in ambuscade for the two brothers. Mārīca was however killed by Rāma and his suspicions being roused, the brothers came back to the hermitage and found that Sītā had been abducted by Rāvaṇa as Jaṭāyu who was still alive told them. Such is probably the unvarnished narrative of Sītā's abduction and is clearly discernible in the poetic account given by the last editor of the *Rāmāyaṇa*.

But how are we to explain the ten heads of Rāvaṇa? And how were they arranged on his shoulders, in a line or a circle? Assuredly he must have had twenty eyes. And how can a being with ten heads and twenty arms be considered an historical being? The plain answer we give is that Rāvaṇa had neither ten heads nor twenty arms nor twenty eyes nor ten necks. The original poem of Vālmīki did not probably represent him as such. The modern idea is one of those curious transformations in which what was once rhetorical becomes by degrees real in popular belief. Gibbon somewhere says "The theory of transubstantiation is rhetoric turned into logic." Rāvaṇa's ten heads seem to have originated in a similar manner. Rāvaṇa had a big head and a big neck as many powerful men have and on account of this fact he was probably originally called दशग्रीव figuratively *i.e.*, a man having a neck as large as ten necks put together. The word ten is often used in this sense and we have another example of it in the *Rāmāyaṇa* itself in the name 'Daśaratha'. Now this word cannot mean that Rāma's father, king of Ayodhyā, had only ten chariots or that he rode in ten chariots at one and the same time.

Perhaps he had a chariot which was as big as ten ordinary chariots or more probably he was a car-warrior equal to ten of his rank. It was thus a name involving a comparison, a simile. In the same way Daśagrīvā or Daśamukha was a name based on a simile. As ages rolled by, the simile was forgotten and Rāvaṇa came to be believed to have had actually ten necks and ten heads.

Many *ślokas* in the *Rāmāyaṇa* probably preserved from the old text support the above theory and show that Rāvaṇa was originally looked upon as having had one head and two arms and two eyes like an ordinary mortal but a larger head and neck than ordinary people have. When Māruti saw Rāvaṇa asleep in his palace we find it stated :

तस्य राक्षसराजस्य निश्चक्राम महामुखात् ।
शयानस्य विनिश्वासः पूरयन्निव तद्गृहम् ।।

Again in another place we have :

नीलजीमूतसंकाशो महाभुजशिरोधरः ।

These *ślokas* show merely that Rāvaṇa had a big head and neck. Then again

काञ्चनाङ्गदसन्नद्धौ ददर्श स महात्मनः ।
निक्षिप्तौ राक्षसेंद्रस्य भुजाविंद्रध्वजोपमौ ।।

Here we have only two arms mentioned and that too when Rāvaṇa was *asleep* and hence had his natural form. The commentator marks the difficulty and explains it under the following *śloka*

ताभ्यां स परिपूर्णाभ्यां भुजाभ्याम् राक्षसेश्वरः ।
शुशुभेऽचलसंकाशः शृङ्गाभ्यामिव मंदरः ।।

भुजद्वयमेव सर्वदा । युद्धादौ स्वेच्छया दशभुजत्वमिति द्विवचनम् । वामदक्षेषु भुजत्वैकवचनमित्यन्ये. If Rāvaṇa had according to the commentator ordinarily two arms and at the time of battle only twenty, then why does it not follow that he had ordinarily one head only ? But if it does not, how are we to explain the following *śloka* where he is said to have two eyes only :

तस्य क्रुद्धस्य नेत्राभ्यां प्रापतन्न श्रुविन्दवः ।
दीपाभ्यामिव दीप्ताभ्यां सार्चिषः स्नेहबिन्दवः ।।

And even in battle he is sometimes represented as having one head only. For only one head is spoken of by Rāma when he says to Rāvaṇa :

अद्य ते मच्छरैश्छिन्नं शिरो ज्वलितकुंडलम् ।
कव्यादा विनिकर्षंतु विकीर्णं रणपांसुषु ॥

But if there is any ambiguity here, there is none where his dead body after death is described. When the widows of Rāvaṇa came to the battle-field, wailing, we find it stated :

उत्क्षिप्य च भुजौ काचिद्भूमौ सुपरिवर्तते ।
हतस्य वदनं दृष्ट्वा काचिन्मोहमुपागता ॥
काचिदंके शिरः कृत्वा रुरोद मुखमीक्षती ॥

Even the गौण or secondary explanation given in the beginning by the commentator of the singular representing a set of ten does not hold good, for the arms and the heads of Rāvaṇa must be supposed to have fallen pell-mell in the battle-field.

It seems, therefore, probable that in individual *ślokas* preserved from the old text, Rāvaṇa is represented as having only one head and two arms though in many places his many arms and heads are distinctly referred to as in the following :

विचित्रं दर्शनीयैश्च रक्ताक्षैर्भीमदर्शनैः ।
शिरोभिर्दशभिर्वीरो भ्राज मानं महौजसम् ॥
बाहुभिर्बद्धकेयूरैश्चन्दनोत्तमरूषितैः ।
भ्राजमानाङ्गदैर्भीमं पंचशीर्षैरिवारेगैः ॥

But passages as these form a strange contrast to those noted above and however much we may try to reconcile them we feel as if the original version of the *Rāmāyaṇa* represented Rāvaṇa as an ordinary human being.

Before concluding this chapter we will refer to another circumstance which makes the story of Sītā's abduction by Rāvaṇa a believable one. It appears probable that among the Rākṣasas the custom of carrying away women for wives prevailed as it does even now among some aboriginal races of India. And it is on this account that this form of marriage is called *rākṣasa* in Sanskrit religious literature as old as the Sūtras. The eight forms of marriage recognised by the Sūtra and Smṛti-writers have different names assigned to them, which are not arbitrary but very probably based on historic grounds. The first four forms *brahma*, *daiva*, *ārṣa* and *prājāpatya* are a gradual development of the idea of marriage as a gift of the girl from religious motives. The *brahma* is the latest development of marriage, being a gift of the bride, pure and simple, with presents and without any conditions. The Prajāpatis were the heads of Aryan families and the form in vogue among them was the gift of the girl on the only stipulation that the bride and bridegroom were to perform the religious duties of a married life. The *daiva* form was that which prevailed amongst the Devas—the remote ancestors of the Aryans of India and the *ārṣa* was the one which prevailed amongst the Ṛṣis, their nearer ancestors. There was a gift in these but not pure and simple as there was some return expected *viz.*, the performance of a sacrifice or the nominal price of two cows. These were developments from a lower form of marriage in which the bride was sold for as much price as the bridegroom could give. This was called the *asura* form as being prevalent amongst the Asuras or the cousins of the remote ancestors of the Aryans. The Rākṣasa was a still lower form in which wives were obtained by force and was so named because it was the form prevalent amongst the Rākṣasas or the cannibal Dravidian aboriginal inhabitants of India. The *gāndharva* form was based on mutual choice and prevailed amongst the Gandharvas who were, as we have elsewhere shown, a race of fair men and women living in the Himalayas and characterised by marital laxity or rather independence. The lowest form was that which prevailed among the Piśācas, a race which fed on human corpses and which was propagated only by acts of sexual intercourse committed by stealth or force as amongst brutes and was therefore named *paiśāca*. These eight forms of marriage are thus the gradual developments of the idea of marriage from mere informal unions to its highest form, the *brahma*, which prevailed amongst the later Aryans of India (the followers of Brahmā) and in which the bride was an irrevocable gift to an unrequiting bridegroom. But what we are concerned with chiefly here is that the names given to these forms are not arbitrary but historical. The *asura* form was really prevalent amongst the Asuras, as we have seen from what is recorded in the *Rāmāyaṇa* and the *Mahābhārata* about the marriages of Kaikeyī and Mādrī. Nay, in the latter case Mādrī's father pleaded the custom of taking bride's price as irrevocable even as regarded a desirable bridegroom and Bhīṣma accordingly had to give rich presents as price. Similarly amongst the Rākṣasas the custom of seizing women by force was the dominant one. It is not strange, therefore, when we find it related that Rāvaṇa had one thousand wives mostly obtained by force and it is not equally strange if he abducted Sītā in a similar way.

XII

THE ALLIANCE WITH THE MONKEYS

Rāma bewailed the loss of his wife with all the vehemence of grief natural to a human being and a loving husband. He wandered through the forest like a mad man calling to his wife every now and then, and often discovering her as if she lay concealed amidst bushes. He now saw what Kaikeyī had meant by his banishment to the Daṇḍakāraṇya and exclaimed, "Now indeed, Kaikeyī ! hast thou accomplished thy object. For I cannot live long nor this Lakṣmaṇa who loves me dearly. Bharata inspite of himself is secured in the enjoyment of the kingdom." From such a disconsolate mood he was roused by Lakṣmaṇa who told him that it was his duty as a man and a husband to hunt out the despoiler of his gem and to kill him, if for nothing else, at least for the sake of the Aryan name. They had come to know from Jaṭāyu that Sītā had been carried away by force by Rāvaṇa, the king of the Rākṣasas, and they set out in search of him gathering information about the country and its people from such persons as they met with in their wanderings. They eventually fell in with Māruti and Sugrīva who had seen Rāvaṇa carry away Sītā in his chariot.

Rāma found in Sugrīva a fellow sufferer and even more. Sugrīva had been expelled by his elder and stronger brother who had also appropriated his fair wife to himself. Sugrīva with his friends, the chief of whom was Hanumān who subsequently became Rāma's greatest friend, lived in a secluded glen of Kiṣkindhā. A compact was soon struck between Sugrīva and Rāma that the latter should assist the former in slaying Vālin and recovering his wife and that Sugrīva when installed king of the monkeys should assist Rāma in finding out Sītā and chastising her captor. The compact was not however entered into before Sugrīva had tested Rāma's power by making him shoot down seven palm trees with one arrow.

The three then set out for the capital of Kiṣkindhā. It was arranged that Sugrīva should invite Vālin to a single combat and Rāma should kill him while fighting with Sugrīva with an arrow. A wreath was bound round the neck of Sugrīva in order that he might be distinguished from his brother.[1] Vālin, a powerful barbarian, came out of the city at the insolent message sent by Sugrīva and accepted a single combat with him not dreaming that there was a third person standing at a great distance who could slay him down from there. A fight ensued between the brothers like a fight between gladiators whose only weapon of offence was their hands. Rāma perceiving that Sugrīva was losing his ground shot an arrow which levelled Vālin to the earth.

Tārā, the wife, and Aṅgada, the son of Vālin, came out from the city weeping for the dying king of monkeys. Vālin

1. A similar contrivance was adopted by Cortez when the people of Cholula were attacked by the Spaniards and their allies, the Tlascalans. "They had bound, by order of Cortez, wreaths of sedge around their heads so that they might more surely be distinguished from the Cholulans." (Prescott, *Conquest of Mexico*, vol. II).

reproached Rāma for his unjustifiable conduct in raising his arm against him without provocation but accepting his fate, requested him to take care of his son. The reply of Rāma in exculpation of his conduct is thus given by Vālmīki. "The earth with all its forests and mountains belongs to the Īkṣvāku race whose duty it is to punish or reward beasts, birds and men according to their deeds. Bharata is the king of that race now and we are his lieutenants and move about the world by his order to establish Dharma. You did a blameworthy action. While Sugrīva is alive you cannot cohabit with Rumā who is his wife and almost your daughter-in-law. He who cohabits with his daughter or sister or daughter-in-law deserves death. The king who does not punish an offence knowing of it, is himself guilty." Rāma in the end comforted the dying Vālin by telling him that Sugrīva who had no son would make Aṅgada his heir-apparent. Rāma then installed Sugrīva in the vacant kingship of Kiṣkindhā. Sugrīva not only thus obtained a kingdom and his wife but also took to wife, Tārā, the beautiful widow of his deceased brother.

Such is the story of Rāma's alliance with Sugrīva who became the king of the monkeys after Vālin was slain by Rāma. Considering it historically, the first question that rises to one's lips is who were the monkeys. They were undoubtedly a human race which was called by that name from their monkeyish appearance. Here we have the same process of transformation of rhetoric into logic. They were also like monkeys, active, ferocious and given up to pleasure. They appear to have used, like the Rākṣasas, nothing but sticks and stones in their fight. Throughout the *Rāmāyaṇa* they are represented as fighting with no other weapons. Of course when the monkeys developed into supernatural beings, stones in the language of hyperbole became huge boulders of rocks and sticks became lofty uprooted trees which were hurled about in battle like chaff. The Aryans who first saw such strange people, wielding no other weapons but stones and sticks, might well have supposed them to be monkeys and the idea once set in motion gained strength by distance and time. Even in the days of Megasthenes people believed in human-beings who covered themselves with their ears or had one leg only. And it is not strange if people even in those days believed that Rāma was assisted by monkeys.

The monkeys thus were human beings, undoubtedly in a low state of civilization. They were, however, strong-minded and strong-bodied and became the allies of the Aryans in their advance against the Rākṣasas probably because they were themselves at enmity with them. They were also not cannibals and their members must frequently have been carried away by Rākṣasas for purposes of food. They were thus thrown willingly into alliance with Rāma against the dreaded Rākṣasas in the same way as the Tlascalans, an aboriginal tribe of Mexico, threw their lot with Cortez and his Spaniards in their contest with the Aztecs. A private feud between Sugrīva and Vālin was the occasion of their alliance in the same way as the feud between the Tlascalans and the Cholulans led to the former invoking the assistance of the Spaniards against the latter with such great benefit to themselves.

We are thus enabled to understand the position of the monkeys in the war of Rāma against the Rākṣasas by what we find of the Tlascalans in the history of the conquest of Mexico. That history will equally supply us with materials for the proper understanding of Rāma's conduct towards Vālin. Apparently Rāma's action seems reprehensible, a dark spot, as it were, on the fair and untarnished glory of this inimitable hero of India. It was this conduct which led Talboys Wheeler to make the strange surmise he makes, when he observes that the truly Vedic story of the Rāma of Ayodhyā ends here and the story of Rāma, the Liṅga-worshipper of the South and the champion of the Hindus against the Buddhists begins. "Rāma the Liṅga-worshipper of the Deccan," he adds "was a different being from the former, unscrupulous in his conduct and not so exalted in character" and that "two distinct traditions referring to different circumstances and localities have been blended together." It is indeed strange to find that such an untenable theory should have been put forward by Talboys Wheeler. But the reason plainly is that he never probably studied the *Rāmāyaṇa* of Vālmīki and derived his information from later versions of Rāma's story. And naturally enough, for even most Hindus do not know that Rāma is not described in the *Rāmāyaṇa* at any place as a Liṅga-worshipper. It would be an astounding revelation to many Hindu readers to know that there is no mention whatever of the founding by Rāma of the great Rāmeśvara Liṅga at the southern extremity of India. This is a story which has very probably been subsequently formulated. There is no doubt a solitary line in the *Rāmāyaṇa* of Vālmīki, when Rāma was returning from Laṅkā and was pointing out to Sītā from his *vimāna* in the sky several places of importance on the earth below as they passed them, wherein it is said :

अत्र प्रसादमकरोन्महादेवः स्वयं मम ।

This line has probably been interpolated in support of the claim of the great temple of Rāmeśvara. It is differently interpreted by the Vaiṣṇavas who see in it nothing of the kind that is ordinarily believed. But leaving that interpretation aside we are bound to state that it was expected that the poet would mention the founding of the Liṅga or even the story of the propitiation of Mahādeva at the time when Rāma was encamped on the coast with his army and was in difficulty as to the crossing of the strait. Moreover Rāma is throughout the length of the *Rāmāyaṇa* of Vālmīki shown as a Vedic Aryan who knew nothing else but *sandhyā* and sacrifice. He is never spoken of as worshipping a Liṅga.[1] And we are constrained to state that the

1. It is Rāvaṇa who is spoken of as worshipping a Liṅga in the Uttarakāṇḍa.

यत्र यत्र च यातिस्म रावणो राक्षसेश्वरः ।
जांबूनदमयं लिंगं तत्र तत्र च नीयते ॥

But even this appears to be a later idea for Rāvaṇa is said to have obtained his *varas* from Brahmā and not Śiva whom he contemptuously treats in his expedition against Kubera. →

very basis of Talboys Wheeler's theory has no existence whatsoever in the *Rāmāyaṇa* of Vālmīki.

Having disposed of Talboys Wheeler's one premiss we will take up the other about the unscrupulousness of Rāma's conduct towards Vālin. The justification which Rāma gives of his own conduct in the poem of Vālmīki, no doubt sounds casuistical but is based on that assumption of universal sovereignty which the Aryans arrogated to themselves in their conscious superiority over the aboriginal races of India. Cortez acted in exactly the same strain when he called upon all Indian caciques to acknowledge the sovereignty of the Spanish Emperor and in default threatened to treat them as rebels to his own sovereign "the rightful lord of these realms" (Prescott, vol. I). It is the right by which stronger and more civilised nations intervene in the concerns of a weaker power on the ground of misrule. Moreover that Vālin was sinful and acting contrary to the practices of his people, nobody will be disposed to doubt. Talboys Wheeler sees no difference between the guilt of Vālin in appropriating the wife of a living brother and the conduct of Sugrīva in taking to wife Tārā, the widow of Vālin. But this difference is actually recognized amongst many castes and aboriginal peoples. It is in fact the story of Hamlet's mother and we have not the least doubt that Rāma's conduct in killing Vālin was justifiable,[1] if not irreproachable. Rāma

कोऽयं शंकर इत्युक्त्वा शैलमूलमुपागतः ।
केन प्रभावेण भवो नित्यं क्रीडति राजवत् ।
विज्ञातव्यं न जानांते भयस्थानमुपागतम् ॥

1. Why Rāma killed Vālin, when he was not fighting with him, has been explained by the poet in another way. Vālin, was a monkey and a human being had by nature a right to hunt a wild animal. In fact Rāma took his stand on the rights of hunting by which he could kill even an innocent and unoffending animal. The explanation is indeed fanciful and based on the assumption that Vālin was really a monkey. Probably Rāma and Sugrīva together fought with Vālin, but supposing the story was originally such as we find it, we can understand Rāma's

after all was a human being and this dark spot only brings out in greater relief the moral sublimity of his conduct throughout the rest of his eventful life.

XIII

THE SIEGE OF LAṄKĀ

Rāma passed the approaching rainy season on a hill near Kiṣkindhā, the capital of Sugrīva, in great anxiety. As soon as the ground was dry enough for movement of the army, he called upon Sugrīva to fulfil his promise by placing at his disposal a sufficient force with which he might hope to conquer his foe. At the command of Sugrīva, their king, thousands of monkeys soon collected at Kiṣkindhā, in numbers which in the hyperbolical language of the *Rāmāyaṇa* could only be counted by billions and trillions. A party of monkeys headed by Hanumān was sent to ascertain if Sītā was really confined in Laṅkā. Hanumān's party soon came to the coast of the southern ocean and there found its further progress stopped by the sea. How to cross the vast expanse of water that separated the Indian continent from the island of Laṅkā was a question which for a time puzzled them. But they soon pitched upon Hanumān "the son of the Wind" as the only being who could accomplish the almost impossible feat of jumping across the strait. Extolled by old Jāmbavān, the great Hanumān soon began to grow in form and assumed a jumping attitude as he sat on a hill on the coast. Larger and larger he grew till at last he seemed a veritable mountain and drawing in his breath he took a powerful jump through the sky across the ocean. The hill propelled back by his feet shot forth trees and flowers as if in ova-

position by remembering that civilised nations even now do not admit the uncivilised races to the same rights in war as are enjoyed by the civilised nations. Had it been otherwise, the Dumdum bullet would have been interdicted in every warfare.

tion of the amazing deed. Māruti flew and flew through the sky, his stupendous shadow running over the surface of the ocean below with the speed of an arrow. At last he reached the opposite coast and took breath having crossed an expanse of the sea— 400 miles in breadth.

Poetically sublime as this scene is, it presents the toughest riddle which an attempt at the historical interpretation of the *Rāmāyaṇa* has to face. Many persons unable to explain how a man can jump across the sea have shifted the scene of operations from Laṅkā to some place on the continent itself. Others believe Laṅkā to be an island in the south of Singapur, while most treat the jump of Māruti as nothing more than the outcome of a poet's imagination. Strangely enough the history of the conquest of Mexico presents us with a parallel which enables us to interpret this event more satisfactorily. The siege of Mexico has graphically been described by Prescott in his great work and we can see thereform how the scene of operation in Mexico resembles the scene of operations in Laṅkā. The city of Mexico was perched on a high table-land to which one ascends from the sea-level by several thousand feet. It was further surrounded by a big lake and was thus cut off entirely from the surrounding mainland, communication with which was kept up only by means of causeways built across the lake. There were bridges at several places in these causeways which when removed, prevented any invader from reaching the city. When the Spaniards who were within the city as friends provoked the rage of the Mexicans by their overbearing conduct and when they fled from it thinking it safe to leave it, the enraged Aztecs pursued them and tried to cut off their retreat by destroying the bridges and breaking the connections. But all the Spaniards succeeded in getting along a causeway to the main land before the bridge was destroyed with the exception of one man named Alvarado. He was now in the grip of the pursuing Aztecs who if they overtook him were sure to sacrifice him to their terrible god. Before him stood a deep and a broad cutting in the causeway which it was impossible for any ordinary human being to jump across. But Alvarado's determination, strength and despair enabled him to accomplish a feat which seemed humanly impossible. "When" writes Prescott, "in the disastrous retreat of the Spaniards, Alvarado cleared a wide gap of the lake at a jump, Aztecs and Tlascalans gazed in stupid amazement exclaiming as they beheld the incredible feat, 'This is truly the Tonateuh, the child of the sun.' The name of 'Alvarado's leap, given to the spot still commemorates an exploit which rivalled those of the demigods of Grecian fable."[1]

It is possible now to understand how Māruti is believed to have jumped across the ocean and also how he came to be looked upon as the 'child of the wind.' It is probable that the island of Laṅkā at some remote time in the past was connected with the main land of India by a chain of rocks, traces of which are still visible at some places. The sea to the left of this chain is deep and makes no sound while that to the right is shallow and always grumbling—a phenomenon which was marked even by Kālidāsa. In this connecting link of rocks there may have been a gap which enabled Rāvaṇa to sleep securely in his capital. Rāvaṇa and his Rākṣasas had probably their own means of crossing this gap like the Aztecs and by removing these means of crossing they could defy an enemy who could not then approach much less invade their island. It was probable that the jumping across such a gap which Māruti attempted and successfully accomplished amazed his friends and foes alike.

Having crossed the sea, Māruti moved towards the city of Laṅkā. The description of the country traversed, the hill on which the city was situated and the city itself as graphically given in the *Rāmāyaṇa* so nearly corresponds with the description of Mexico given by Prescott that we are tempted to give it here in detail. "As he approached the opposite coast, Māruti beheld an island adorned with

1. *Conquest of Mexico*, vol. II, p. 314.

diverse kinds of trees and forests of sandal-wood. He beheld in one view the sea, its curving coast line, the luxuriant vegetation fringing it and the mouths of the various rivers as they kissed the sea. Alighting on the coast he crossed green open lands interspersed with hills and sweet smelling forests full of honey. The powerful monkey then ascended a chain of mountains covered with thick jungles full of full-blossomed trees. Reaching the top of the range, he saw Laṅkā perched on the top of a hill and surrounded by gardens and natural groves." This description of the landscape as given by Vālmīki corresponds exactly with the description of the land of the Aztecs as given by Prescott. There we have first the *tiera* Calienta "a broad tract along the Atlantic full of sandy plains intermingled with others of luxuriant fertility impervious from thickets of aromatic shrubs, from the middle of which tower up trees of magnificent growth. Then sweeping along the base of lofty mountains, the traveller mounts into the *tiera* Templada, thickly covered with forest-trees in the days of the Aztecs." And going higher up he sees the city of Mexico situated on the Terra Firma on the table-land at the top of the Cordilleras. The vast lake which surrounded the city of Mexico on all sides and formed one of its great defences has alone no counterpart in Laṅkā. But its place is taken up by the straits which lie between Ceylon and India and which form, as it were, a big moat around the northern part of the island.

Māruti gazed with wonder at the city of Laṅkā, surrounded as it was with a golden wall with four gates. This statement seems at first sight fabulous and untrue. But there undoubtedly lies under it a substratum of truth. When we remember what a vast amount of gold the Mexicans had in their possession, when we read that in Peru there was a big temple of the Sun, the walls of which were coated with plates of solid gold, when we find that the now exposed city of Lhasa possesses a temple situated on a hill the roof of which is covered with gold, we cannot but grant that the Rākṣasas, with an ingenuity and a liking peculiar to the barbarians, had really ornamented the wall of their city, at least here and there, with golden plates. That they must have possessed gold in abundance seems very probable. Southern India and Laṅkā in former times were full of gold which was found in the sands of their rivers and in their mines and gold is even now plentifully found in the mines worked in the Mysore State. The fabulous golden Laṅkā therefore seems to us to be only an exaggeration and not a mere creation of the poet's brain.

Māruti entered the city quietly and saw large and beautiful palaces in the construction of which the inhabitants had exhibited the same gorgeousness. The description which the poet gives of the palaces of Rāvaṇa surpasses even our imagination. The Royal palatial ground occupied a space about three miles in circumference, an extent not at all too much when placed by the side of the extent recorded of the palaces of Montezuma "the terraced roof of which might have afforded ample room for thirty knights to run their courses in a regular tournament." Māruti entered the inner apartments of Rāvaṇa's palace fearlessly, probably with a view to see if Sītā was to be found there, perhaps with that privilege which belongs to every poet and historian. He saw there one thousand beautiful women all asleep. They had mostly been brought together by force; though there were some who had come to Rāvaṇa smitten with love. There is probably no exaggeration here also, for Montezuma, Rāvaṇa's prototype, had also one thousand wives "whom he had taken away by force from their weeping parents." The Spaniards everywhere heard complaints about the "unfeeling manner in which Montezuma carried away maidens for his harem." Leaving the harem Māruti wandered over the whole palace with its gorgeous equipment in search of Sītā and not finding her there entered Rāvaṇa's gardens beautified by well constructed paths and abounding in ponds full of lotuses. The whole picture is perhaps too highly coloured by "the proneness to exaggerate which was natural to those who first witnessed a spectacle so striking the imagination, so new and unexpected." But there is a vein of truth in all this hyperbolical description though it may appear at this distance of time and in the totally altered circumstances of our day as unreal or imaginary.

Māruti found Sītā sitting under a tree in the Aśoka grove of the garden, pale, emaciated and mournful. Judging her to be the great queen of Rāma he slowly appeared before her and with a view to convince her that he was not an enemy threw Rāma's ring into her sight. Overpowered with joy at the sudden sight of the ring, beyond all expectation, beyond all hope Sītā gazed at Māruti for a long time while tears of joy flowed down her cheeks copiously. He then explained to her how and why he had come there and comforted her with the assurance that Rāma would come soon with a mighty army to rescue her. She was overjoyed and happy and thought she had not lived in vain that long life of misery. "Joy does come to a living being even though after years of pain and misery," she exclaimed and sent word with him to Rāma that she was faithful and alive, and hoped that she would be united with her loving husband at no distant date after Rāvaṇa with the whole of his cannibal host had been killed and annihilated. She, however, warned him that Rāvaṇa had allowed her one year (which was drawing to a close) to reconcile herself to her situation and had threatened to kill her at the end of that period.

Māruti took from her a memento in return and leaving the city by daybreak returned to Bhārata by the same route. He duly returned to Kiṣkindhā and gave the welcome news of his discovery of Sītā in Laṅkā and her message to Rāma. The despairing husband pressed him to his chest as his greatest friend and extolled his power and greatness to the skies.

Rāma now moved with his army of monkeys (perhaps called by that name by the Rākṣasas in their overbearing confidence in themselves in the same contemptuous way as the Russians at the beginning of the last war called the

Japanese 'yellow monkeys') and soon came to the seacoast. He was joined there by Vibhīṣaṇa, a brother of Rāvaṇa, who was disgusted with his proud behaviour. Vibhīṣaṇa plays the same part in the war with the Rākṣasas as Ixtlilchitl, a prince of the Aztec race, who gave up the cause of the Mexicans and joined the Spaniards in their attack on the city of Mexico. We always find in history that uncivilised and backward races as a rule lose by the defection of their own members. Rāvaṇa was incensed at the conduct of his brother and gave utterance to a *śloka* which at all times and in all climes has an interest of its own. "We are reminded" said he, "of what the elephants say in the forests. 'We fear none but our own brethren.' "[1]

The difficulty of taking a large army over the gap of the sea confronted Rāma at this point. Boats could not be thought of in a rough and shallow sea and in front of a determined enemy if he chose to act in time. The difficulty was however got over in the same way as it was got over by the Spaniards. The Bhārata allies were made to fill up the canals and ditches with stones, earth and whatever else they could lay their hands on and as they pulled down the buildings the Aztecs said in scorn "go on fools, go on, if we conquer you will have to build them again for us; if the Spaniards, you will have to build for them." But Rāvaṇa and his Rākṣasas unlike the Aztecs did not watch the filling of the gap by the monkeys with stones; and slept unmindful of the danger that was overtaking them in over-estimation of the strength of their natural defences. The indefatigable monkeys worked day and night and filled up the gap and the army of monkeys with Rāma and Lakṣmaṇa at their head safely crossed over the ocean and encamped before the city of Laṅkā in four divisions before its four gates.

The description of the siege of Laṅkā as given in the *Rāmāyaṇa* resembles the description of the siege of Mexico

1. It seems that the device of catching elephants by the aid of tame elephants is an ancient one.

as given by Prescott or in fact of every other city which in spite of heroic resistance has been successfully besieged in the history of the world. We have the same story of sallies made from the different gates, generally ineffectual and often attended with the death of the commander. The population of the city gradually found itself starved and without ammunition. There were general assaults on the walls of the city by the monkeys which were very often repelled with great loss and slaughter on both sides. Eventually a conflagration in a part of the city caused general disorder and despair and failure of food and ammunition foreshadowed either capitulation or a successful storming of the city. Rāvaṇa, however, with the same dogged determination and barbarous ferocity as characterised the Aztecs and their young King Gnatemozin the son-in-law and successor of Montezuma fought till the bitter end. Commander after commander fell in the sorties ordered by him. It would be needless to enter into the details of these events but we might mention how Rāvaṇa's son Indrajit and his brother Kumbhakarṇa fell. Indrajit is supposed to have once almost killed the two brothers by his skilful handling of the bow and when he was on the point of finishing a sacrifice by means of which he hoped to obtain a chariot on which he was to ride to battle invincible, he was surprised and killed by Lakṣmaṇa who was taken to the place of the sacrifice by Vibhīṣaṇa. We have already said that the Rākṣasas though ferocious were uncivilized barbarians. It is, therefore, the imagination of later poets which depicts them as using the bow or as sacrificing in the Aryan fashion with Vedic *mantras*. We have already stated that the great weapon of the Aryans at this time was the bow and the arrow as that of the Spaniards was the cannon and the ball. Superiority of weapons is one of the most obvious causes which has always led to the triumph of a higher civilization over a lower. All the Rākṣasas with the exception of Indrajit and Rāvaṇa are represented as fighting with sticks, tridents and javelins like the Aztecs of Mexico. We may believe that Indrajit scored some success over the brothers for a time or that the local knowledge of Vibhīṣaṇa enabled Lakṣmaṇa to discover and kill him as he lay in ambuscade. But he had no bow nor did he sacrifice with Vedic rites. Kumbhakarṇa similarly depended on his huge size and strength when he issued out of the northern gate in a sally. He is represented as having used first a *triśūla* and latterly his arms only. Rāma succeeded in cutting off his arms and legs and the huge Rākṣasa fell down dead crushing as the poet describes, to death several of the enemy by the mere weight and dimensions of his body.

His brother and son, two greatest warriors on whom he relied killed, his army shattered, his city in flames and his subjects crying and cursing him, Rāvaṇa the king of cannibals, was now at his wits' ends. Burning with rage and despair he thought with a cannibal's instinct of killing poor Sītā who was the cause of all that misery and taking a sword with him he went to her place of confinement. Her great beauty however and the admonition of his minister succeeded in diverting the dread king from his fell design and he resolved upon making his last and greatest effort for killing his inveterate foe before he destroyed with his own hands his precious prize. Hundreds and thousands of Rākṣasas headed by the enraged Rāvaṇa now issued out of the northern gate and a terrible battle ensued which lasted for a long time. Rāvaṇa is said to have used a bow and arrows but he is represented as wounding Lakṣmaṇa with a heavy javelin. Lakṣmaṇa was taken off the field of battle and tended with care[1] and the battle still raged on. The fight was unparalleled in the history of the ancient Aryans of India. As the poet has said, "The fight of

1. It is stated that Lakṣmaṇa was brought round and saved from the effects of his mortal wounds by the use of Sañjīvanī herb which grew on a mountain-top in the Himalayas which Māruti brought bodily from there to Laṅkā on his hand through the sky. The scene is thrice repeated in the *Rāmāyaṇa* and can only be explained as an emanation from the poetical imagination of the last editor who wished to heap marvels in the wonderful story of Rāma's war with the Rākṣasas.

Rāma and Rāvaṇa has its like in itself." At last the terrible Rākṣasa king with his heart pierced by an arrow from Rāma fell down dead to the great joy and relief of gods, mortals and monkeys leaving the untold riches of the gold-walled Laṅkā, a prize to the immortal victor.

Such is the story of the siege of Laṅkā and Rāvaṇa's death, a story which in its unvarnished simplicity is marvellous enough. It is not strange that indigestible exaggeration should have gathered about it in the course of thousands of years which have elapsed since then. Nay, from what we read of the exaggerations which had gathered round Montezuma during his own life-time, it is possible that even during Rāma's own life the story of his fight with Rāvaṇa and the greatness of Rāvaṇa's power and Laṅkā's wealth must have been distorted and inflated with the most extraordinary pomp and circumstance. What people in India believe about Rāvaṇa at this day ages after he has passed away, people believed of Montezuma in his own days ! "You too", said he with a smile to the Spaniards "have been told that I am a god and dwell in palaces of gold and silver. But you see it is false; my houses though large are of stone and wood like those of others. And as to my body" he said barring his tawny arm "it is bone and flesh like yours." It is a pity but it is also a gain that these words of Montezuma enable us to divest Rāvaṇa and Laṅkā of their amazing but exaggerated grandeur.

Even if we divest Rāvaṇa and Laṅkā of their unreal greatness the achievement of Rāma in invading and conquering Laṅkā cannot but strike us as stupendous. The ancient Aryans of India were animated by a spirit of adventure like their brethren of the west. And though the races with whom they came into contact were undoubtedly in a low state of civilization, though in fact the Rākṣasas were bound to fall, as all lower races have fallen for the two reasons already noticed viz., the inferiority of arms and the inferiority of political morality as evidenced by divisions and defection yet the leaders of the Aryans must have possessed unflinching courage, never failing resource and unbounded confidence in themselves before they could have conquered a whole nation of fierce cannibals. And when we take into consideration the sublime character which set off these qualities in Rāma, we cannot but admire a hero higher than Cortez or any of those adventurers in modern history who sometimes dived single-handed into unknown regions peopled by unknown races and by their will and energy rose to fame and fortune.

XIV

THE PAINFUL SEQUEL

Triumphant Rāma now ordered Vibhīṣaṇa to perform the obsequies of the great king of the Rākṣasas observing that his enmity ceased with his enemy's death. He then asked Lakṣmaṇa to have sea water brought in golden jars and seating Vibhīṣaṇa on the vacant throne of Laṇkā, he poured the holy water on his head consecrating him king of that country. Having thus rewarded his ally he next thought of the long suffering Sītā and sent Hanumān to apprise her of the death of her tormentor and the victory of her husband. The poor forlorn woman felt as if she was alive again and in her joy she was sorry she had nothing to give to Hanumān in return for the happiest news he had brought to her. She said she wished to see her lord from whom she had so long and so painfully been separated. Rāma on hearing the message thus sent with Hanumān at once asked Vibhīṣaṇa to get her duly bathed and anointed and to have her brought with due decorum. In a few hours a palanquin escorted by Rākṣasas appeared and Vibhīṣaṇa directed his mace-bearers to remove the crowd that surrounded Rāma. But Rāma interposed saying that a woman's appearance in public was not blamable at the time of a sacrifice, a marriage or a great calamity. He asked Vibhīṣaṇa to bring Sītā before him on foot so that all his friends might have an opportunity of seeing her. Lakṣmaṇa and Hanumān, Vibhīṣaṇa and Sugrīva were pained to hear these words spoken by Rāma and Sītā too with her heart failing within her came and stood in front of him. With mingled feelings of joy, wonder and affection, the devoted wife gazed at her dear husband's face. But in that countenance the feelings of shame and rage alternately appeared and Rāma slowly said "Here art thou, O Sītā, conquered back from my enemy. I have done what a brave man ought to do and have together wiped off my enemy and my disgrace. I have fulfilled my vow and rescued thee from confinement. The great deed of Hanumān in jumping across the sea and entering Laṅkā alone has indeed borne fruit now and so indeed have the valour of Sugrīva and the friendship of Vibhīṣaṇa. But remember all this was done in order to vindicate my honour and the honour of the great sun-race. As to thee thy sight does not please me now as that of a lamp does not him whose eyes are sore. Go wherever it pleases thee for what honourable man will take back a wife defiled by a long stay in another's house." These words fell like a thunder bolt on the ears of the unhappy woman and she felt as if life was passing away from her but slowly summoning up courage she replied "Wherefore dost thou utter these harsh words treating me as a worthless man treats his worthless wife? I swear and am ready to prove that I am pure. I was indeed touched by Rāvaṇa but I was helpless. I am doomed indeed beyond remedy if my life-long devotion to thee established during a contact of years was not sufficient to convince thee how my mind is pure. Influenced by rage thou lookest upon me as an ordinary woman and settest no value on the sacred grasp of my hand at the time of marriage, my devotion, my character." With tears rolling down her pale cheeks she said to Lakṣmaṇa, "Raise me a pyre of faggots. I cannot live in the face of such unfounded accusation. The only course open to me, abandoned as I am by my displeased husband in public, is to burn myself in fire." Lakṣmaṇa in his anguish looked at Rāma but finding that he was not opposed to that course at once had a pile of faggots brought and set on fire. Rāma held down his head as Sītā going round him made her last bow to him and approaching the fire said, "As I am pure at heart and always devoted to Rāma, may this fire protect me on all sides; as Rāma thinks me defiled though I am pure, may this fire protect me on all sides" and then with the courage of a devoted wife she threw herself into the pile of burning wood. A cry of horror rose from the assembled crowd of men and women and Rāma with tears starting from his eyes looked up. But god Fire brought Sītā unscathed out of the burning pile and told Rāma that she was pure and sinless. Monkeys and Rākṣasas saw the great ordeal. Rāma received back his wife with joy observing that it was necessary that his wife who had lived so long at the house of the unscrupulous Rākṣasa king should perform an ordeal before he could take her back.

Such was the great ordeal which Sītā performed in order to prove her sinlessness. Whether such ordeals are possible or not we will not pause to discuss; for in spite of that ordeal people doubted even in Rāma's time whether Sītā was pure or not and down to this day historians like Talboys Wheeler raise the same doubt. There are, however, strong reasons which go to convince us that Sītā was never forcibly defiled by Rāvaṇa. The last editor of the *Rāmāyaṇa* has put in two different stories *viz.*, that of Nalakubera's curse and the curse of Brahmā to explain why Rāvaṇa was prevented from compelling Sītā, a mere woman, by force to be his wife. Why Rāvaṇa did not take such a course can be explained however on a more historical basis. We have already shown that it was a custom among the Rākṣasas to forcibly seize and carry away women for wives. But it was also a custom among them that when the wife of a living man was carried away by force, she was allowed a period of one year to reconcile herself to her new condition and in order to allow her husband an opportunity to rescue her by killing or defeating her captor. We find it stated in the *Mahābhārata* that in the *rākṣasa* form of marriage, the woman ought to be allowed a period of one year before she is taken to bed. It is curious to find in the *Rāmāyaṇa* that Rāvaṇa allows the same period to Sītā to reconcile herself to her new condition. And it appears certain that even if Rāma had not succeeded in rescuing her within one year, Rāvaṇa would not have compelled her to be his wife against her will but with the strange love of a cannibal and a Rākṣasa would have cut her up and eaten her flesh, as he actually threatens to do in one of his love speeches to Sītā. Among the Aztecs, we read that a man who was to be offered in sacrifice to their terrible god was attended upon by several young ladies for the period of one year and was then sacrificed and his flesh was eaten up perhaps by those very women who were his associates. In fine, cannibals had strange customs of their own and it does not seem probable that Rāvaṇa would have acted in direct opposition to that custom among them which prohibited the defiling of a captive woman against her will.

United with his beloved and loving wife, Rāma returned to Ayodhyā in company of Sugrīva and Vibhīṣaṇa, his allies and their great nobles. It must have taken him several months to accomplish the journey even with the facilities which two such powerful kings could afford.[1] The joy of Bharata knew no bounds when he saw Rāma return safe and, as he now knew, victorious from a sanguinary war. He showed him the way in which he had administered the kingdom during his absence, like an honest steward by increasing the treasury tenfold and he then put the golden sandals on to Rāma's feet saying that he returned the kingdom entrusted to him to its rightful owner. The meeting between Rāma and Lakṣmaṇa and their mothers, between the people and their rightful Lord and now raised

1. The idea that Rāma went back to Ayodhyā in one day in a *vimāna* of Kubera strikes us as hyperbolical. But it is possible to believe that he was carried in a palanquin of superb construction by fast bearers, a palanquin, given by Vibhīṣaṇa and resembling that used by Montezuma richly decorated with plates of gold and precious stones having pillows curiously wrought and supporting a canopy of green plumes.

to the summit of fame by his conquest of Laṅkā may better be imagined than described. Vasiṣṭha, the aged preceptor of the family without delay performed the coronation ceremony of Rāma seated with his beauteous and devoted wife Sītā on a golden throne and placed on his head the ancient crown of Ayodhyā which had come down from the days of Manu, amidst unbounded rejoicings. Sītā gave to Hanumān a necklace from her own neck in memento of the happy event which was almost impossible but for his great sacrifices. Suitable rewards and presents were given to the other guests who thereafter returned to their respective kingdoms in the South.

Rāma was now supremely happy but his happiness lasted only a few months. Sītā was now pregnant and according to Indian custom he asked her what thing she most liked. She replied that she would like to spend one day among the Brahmin settlements on the banks of the Ganges. Rāma promised to fulfil her wish and as he came out of the palace and asked as usual for news, his reporters told him that the people were all happy under his rule and extolled his great exploits but that they wondered how Rāma derived pleasure in the company of a wife who had been defiled by a long stay in Rāvaṇa's house. A great man's conduct, they said, was an example for others and they were expected to follow that ? It was the old story or rather the ever recurring story. Sītā's abduction by Rāvaṇa had forever poisoned the cup of Rāma's remaining life. Rāma breathed hard and heaved long but having determined upon the course to be taken called his brothers. With tears in his eyes he told them to do what he ordered without remonstrance if they loved him. He told them what people thought of his wife and himself and of the action he was going to take in consequence. He would give up his wife, even his brothers, even his own life to please and satisfy the people. He then asked Lakṣmaṇa to take Sītā next morning to the Brahmin hermitages on the other side of the Ganges—fortunately she had already expressed a wish to go there—and to abandon her there altogether.

Next morning saw Sītā accompanied by Lakṣmaṇa seated in a chariot running wildly through the city of Ayodhyā towards the Ganges. Poor Sītā could not understand why Lakṣmaṇa's eyes were blood-red. "Why dost thou grieve so much" said the unsuspecting Sītā, "I too feel sad for being separated from the broad-chested Rāma; but we will return tomorrow after giving these valuable clothes and ornaments to poor Brahmin ladies." Lakṣmaṇa could not utter a single word, his throat being choked with tears. At last they were on the banks of the Ganges and were soon ferried across by the fishermen. Then Lakṣmaṇa fell at Sītā's feet and with hot tears flowing from his eyes he said, "Pardon me, O blameless qeeen, for what I am doing. I am ordered to abandon you here, for the people blame Rāma for keeping you in his house." It was too much even for the long suffering Sītā and she fell down insensible. When Lakṣmaṇa brought her round with the Ganges water she cried long and bitterly. At last she said "I do not know what sin I committed in my former life or which man I separated from his wife. I lived in the Daṇḍakāraṇya for years but Rāma was then with me. How shall I live now without him ? I would indeed have destroyed myself but for this precious burden which I bear in my womb. Go Lakṣmaṇa go, obey thou the command of the king. And tell him my message, 'You know me pure and devoted but abandon me in deference to the people's wish. It is my duty to acquiesce in this that scandal may not sully your great name. A husband is to a woman her god, her preceptor, her friend and she should do what pleases her husband even at the cost of her own life.' " Lakṣmaṇa bowed to her and advising her to take shelter in Vālmīki's hermitage left her with a wrench of his exhausted feelings.

Rāma engaged his unhappy mind in righteously ruling his subjects and in performing a number of Aśvamedha sacrifices. Years passed away when during one sacrificial session his attention was drawn by the singing of two beautiful Brahmin boys. He called them to him, looked at them minutely and heard their singing with a rivetted ear. His heart began to yearn towards them and inquiring who they were he came to know that they were his twin-born sons by Sītā and brought up by Vālmīki who had come there for the performance of the sacrifice. Rāma was now deeply excited, and anxious to be reunited with his beloved wife. He sent message to Vālmīki that he would like Sītā to swear her innocence in the great assemblage of Ṛṣis and princes, monkeys and Rākṣasas who had come to assist in and witness the performance of his Aśvamedha sacrifice. Next morning accordingly a great concourse of men, Ṛṣis, princes and citizens assembled in the sacrificial hall. In anxious expectation the concourse became stony and motionless as behind Vālmīki walked the trembling and emaciated Sītā with hands folded in adoration and thinking of Rāma alone. "Great is Rāma" cried some, "great is Sītā" said others. When she was in front of Rāma Vālmīki said, "Oh son of Daśaratha, here is Sītā whom you abandoned in consequence of public disapprobation. She will now swear her purity if permitted by you. Here are your twin-born sons bred up by me in my hermitage." "I know" said Rāma "that Sītā is pure and that these are my sons. She performed an ordeal in Laṅkā in proof of her purity and therefore I took her back. But people here have doubts still so let Sītā perform an ordeal here so that all these Ṛṣis and people may witness it. With eyes cast down on the ground and with hands folded, Sītā swore. "As I never thought of any man except Rāma even in my mind let Mother Earth open and take me in. As I always loved Rāma in words, in thoughts, and in deed let Mother Earth open and take me." As she uttered the oath, the earth verily opened and Sītā was carried away inside seated on a golden *siṁhāsan!* Heavenly flowers fell on Sītā's head while the audience looked on as in a trance. Rāma with his head hanging down and tears running down his cheeks stood motionless long clutching his wand, till at last over-powered with rage and grief he cried "Give back, Mother Earth, give back my Sītā; or else take me within thee sothat I may live long with her in the recesses of thy heart." "Give back, Mother Earth, my Sītā," said he again "whom I brought back from Laṅkā, or else I will harass thee from ocean to ocean." When he came to himself he dismissed the sages assembled and sought refuge in a cottage of leaves erected on the sacrificial ground.

Rāma was now irrevocably separated from his wife and must soon have become wearied of life and the world. With that religious contempt for life which the Aryans of India of by-gone days exhibited, he must have soon resolved upon *mahāprasthāna*. When life's duty was done or when its pleasure was gone, the ancient Aryans did not cling to life with greater fondness but they took the vow of *vānaprastha* or *sannyāsa* passing the remainder of their life in religious contemplation; or the more heroic performance what is known in the Dharmaśāstras as the *mahāprasthāna*. They did not wait for death but started on their way towards it and met it half ways. Both Rāma and Yudhiṣṭhira are said to have thus gone forth on their last pilgrimage, contemptuously declining to die at home of disease or decay. The *Rāmāyaṇa* of Vālmīki says that every living being in Ayodhyā including man, woman and beast accompanied Rāma when he set out from Ayodhyā and as they bathed in the Sarayū they were all transported to heavens by Rāma's favour.

Kuśa and Lava, the sons of Rāma, ruled in Kuśāvatī and Śrāvastī after Rāma's death in kingdoms of the same name, Ayodhyā having disappeared entirely. Many modern Rajput races derive their descent from these sons of Rāma, the chief of them being the Suśodias of Mewar whose king is believed in India to have sprung, in an unbroken line through Kuśa.

APPENDICES

1.

THE EXTENT OF THE *RĀMĀYAṆA* AND ITS BOMBAY AND BENGAL VERSIONS

The Bombay edition of the *Rāmāyaṇa* has got the following *śloka* in the beginning of the Bālakāṇḍa

चतुर्विंशत्सहस्राणि श्लोकानामुक्तवानृषिः ।
तथा सर्गशतान्पंच षट्काण्डानि सहोत्तरम् ।।

We thus find that the *Rāmāyaṇa* declares its own contents to be 24,000 *ślokas* divided into 500 *sargas* or chapters put under six *kāṇḍas* or sub-divisions with the addition of a seventh named the Uttarakāṇḍa or subsequent book. The Bengal or Gouda version called by the name of Gorresio's edition is believed by some, notably Mr. Abhyankar who has written an excellent brochure in Marathi on the *Rāmāyaṇa*, to have no Uttarakāṇḍa and as a matter of fact in the text printed by Gorresio the Uttarakāṇḍa is not found. But it is apprehended that this is so because that *kāṇḍa* in that version is now lost and not because it did not exist at all. For in the Ādikāṇḍa (as Bālakāṇḍa is named therein) we find a chapter giving the extent and contents of the poem and the number of the *ślokas* and chapters in each *kāṇḍa*. That number is as follows and it nearly coincides with the table of contents given in the Bombay edition.

Name of *kāṇḍa*	No. of chapters	No. of *ślokas*
Ādikāṇḍa	64	2850
Ayodhyā	80	4170
Araṇya	114	4150
Kiṣkindhā	64	2925
Sundara	43	2045
Yuddha	105	4500
Abhyudayika	90	3360
(अभ्युदयिकं सभविष्यं सहोत्तरम्)		
	560	24000

This clearly shows that the Uttarakāṇḍa was there in Gorresio's text. Moreover if the Uttarakāṇḍa had no existence in that version, it is difficult to explain how in the beginning the song is said to be sung by Kuśa and Lava, the sons of Rāma, who had been taught by Vālmīki. As we have said in the body of the book, the Uttarakāṇḍa is at least as old as the last compilation of the *Rāmāyaṇa* because Kālidāsa gives an epitome of it in his *Raghuvaṁśa* and often in the same words. It appears that Mr. Abhyankar is mistaken when he says that the Uttarakāṇḍa has no existence in the Bengal version and we believe that that version has only lost that *kāṇḍa*. It appears also probable that this bifurcation of the poem into two versions is much posterior to the last compilation of the poem in 100 B.C. which date we have arrived at on the strength of the fact that the कच्चित् chapter in the Ayodhyākāṇḍa and the geographical chapters in the Kiṣkindhā taking their starting point, absurdly enough, from the Kurukshetra instead of from Kiṣkindhā, are interpolations made by the last compiler in imitation of the *Mahābhārata*. Both these chapters are found in Gorresio's edition. The *śloka* giving the auspicious conjunctions of the planets in *rāśis* at the time of Rāma's birth and the one which contains a direct condemnation of Buddha are not found (as Mr. Abhyankar has pointed out) in this edition and these *ślokas* might have, therefore, been introduced in the Bombay edition still later. As a matter of fact we have already noticed in the body of the book that the *Rāmāyaṇa* is being added to all along.

It is suggested by Mr. Abhyankar that Gorresio's text is the older and the more reliable of the two. We have already stated that this division of text and arrangement took place after the last compilation of the *Rāmāyaṇa* had been made about 100 B.C. In both countries *viz.*, Bengal and Southern India this last compilation was subsequently subjected here and there to prunings and minor additions. But we believe that while more additions have heen made in the South, in Bengal the text has been pruned with more liberty. We took the trouble of looking into the Bengal text to see how many of the *ślokas* which preserve ideas older than the last compilation and on which we have based much of our criticism in both its parts, can be found in that text. And strangely enough we found that many of these *ślokas* have been pruned and corrected in the Bengal text, so as to come into line with modern feeling. We give below these *ślokas*, for the sake of comparison.

ĀDI OR BĀLAKĀṆḌA

1. दशवर्षसहस्राणि दशवर्षशतानि च ।
रामो राज्यमुपासित्वा ब्रह्मलोकं प्रयास्यति ॥

is found in both.

2. When Nārada in the first *sarga* tells Rāma's story in short to Vālmīki the Bengal text adds

नारदस्य तु तद्वाक्यं श्रुत्वा वाक्यविशारदः ।
वाल्मीकिः शिष्यसहितो विस्मयं परमं ययौः ॥

This clearly shows that Vālmīki did not know Rāma's story.

3. मा निषाद प्रतिष्ठां त्वमगमः etc. is found in both.

4. Brahmā says to Vālmīki

वृत्तं प्रथय रामस्य यथा ते नारदाच्छ्रुतम् ।
सर्वं विदितमेतत्ते मत्प्रसादाद्भविष्यति ।
वैदेह्याश्चैव यद्वृत्तं प्रकाशं यदि वा रहः ॥

This strengthens the idea that Vālmīki did not know Rāma's story as also the following *śloka*

श्रुत्वा पूर्वं काव्यबीजं देवर्षेर्नारदादृषिः ॥
लोकादन्विष्य भूयश्च चरितं चरितव्रतः ॥

5. The subjects of the Uttarakāṇḍa in the chapter of table of contents are given as follows :

राक्षसानां समुत्पत्ति रावणस्य जयं तथा ।
सीतायाश्च परित्यागं प्रकृतीनां च रंजनम् ॥
प्राप्तराज्यस्य रामस्य चरितं यच्च श्रीमतः ।
अथागमनमृषीणां च शत्रुघ्नस्य विसर्जनम् ।
वने प्रसूतिं सीताया लवणस्य रणे वधम् ॥
कालदुर्वाससोः प्राप्तिः लक्ष्मणस्य विसर्जनम् ।
स्थापयित्वा यथा पुत्रान् रामो राज्ये दिवं गतः ॥

6. The extent of the *Rāmāyaṇa* is given as 24,000 *ślokas*, the same as in the Bombay edition.

चतुर्विंशतिसाहस्रं सर्वपापभयावहम् ।

7. Śāntā and Ṛṣyaśṛṅga *ākhyānas* come before the advice of Vasiṣṭha. This is a correction over the Bombay edition. But the *putreṣṭi* sacrifice all the same seems to be superfluous as the Ṛṣis who performed the Aśvamedha, when they left, promised four sons to Daśaratha.

8. Kausalyā killing the sacrificial horse with three strokes of her sword has been changed. This is an improvement over the original text.

कौसल्या तं हयं तत्र परिगम्य प्रदक्षिणम्
अध्वर्युसहिता चैनं समालभ्य शुचिव्रता ॥
रजनीं पर्युपास्तैका कोशल्या पुत्रकाम्यया

9. Rāma was born of half the spirit of Viṣṇu as in the Bombay text विष्णोर्वीर्यार्द्धतो जज्ञे रामो राजीवलोचनः.

10. The *śloka* in the Bombay edition which betrays the interpolated nature of the *ślokas* and gives Sītā's age of marriage as six (see Appendix 6) is pruned in the

Bengal text in deference to the prevailing custom of child marriage in Bengal

अभिवाद्याभिवाद्यांश्च तत्र पूज्यान् गुरूंस्ततः ।
रेमिरे मुदितास्तत्र भर्तृप्रियहिते रताः ।।

11. Ahalyā's story is the same. She is not transformed into a stone.

तप्यमाना निरालंबा सततं भूमिशायिता । (Ayodhyākāṇḍa)

12. Daśaratha is said to be अनेकवर्षशतिकः वृद्धोस्यद्य नरेश्वर. This is less hyperbolical than वर्षाणामयुतं ययौ.

13. Kausalyā is not performing a sacrifice when Rāma sees her

ददर्श याचमानां तु देवतावेश्मनि श्रियम् ।
प्राणायामेन पुरुषं ध्यायन्ती सा जनार्दनम् ।।

This is perfectly modern as also the following

अकरोत्प्रयता पूजां देवानां नियतव्रता ।

14. The extremely interesting *śloka* about Rāma having many wives is suitably pruned

ऋद्धियुक्ता श्रिया जुष्टा रामपत्नी भविष्यति ।
कल्याणि त्वसमृद्धा हि स्नुषा ते च भविष्यति ।।

15. Rāma's character, when he sees Sītā after the order for his banishment is represented as more stern. ततो विवृततां गतः is not to be found.

16. आर्यपुत्र कथं चीरमहं बध्नामि शंस मे is less poetical than in the other text and she puts the garment on herself.

17. Sītā's prayer to the Ganges as she crosses it, is a change from a propitiation by *sura* to one by sacrifice.

18. The long-metred *śloka* about the Vatsas after the contradictory preceding line अद्य दुःखं तु वैदेही वनवासस्य वेत्स्यति is not found in Gorresio's text.

19. The interpolated *sarga* containing the famous *śloka* त्वदर्थमिव विन्यस्तः शिलापट्टोऽयमग्रतः quoted by Bhavabhūti and the काक and इषीकास्त्र stories are found in this text also. This probably shows that divergence of text took place after Bhavabhūti.

20. The कच्चित् chapter is found but is not followed by

प्रष्टं समुपचक्रमे but by Bharata telling straight the news of Daśaratha's death. लक्ष्मण उवाच is hereafter strangely added contrary to the general way of introducing speeches in the *Rāmāyaṇa* which does not use this form but has a *śloka* instead.

21. Jābāli gives the same tirade against religion and *śrāddha*.

22. The *śloka* about बुद्ध is not found.

23. The *śloka* which refers to the वराह Avatāra is suitably changed in this text. Instead of ततःसमभवद्ब्रह्मा स्वयंभूर्दैवतैःसह we have ततः समभवद्ब्रह्मा स्वयंभूर्विष्णुरव्ययः and then follows

स वराहोथ भूत्वेमामुज्जहार वसुंधराम् ।
असृजच्च जगत्सर्वं सचराचरमव्ययम् ।।

24. The story of *pādukas* being given to Bharata is somewhat different. Śarabhaṅga sent कुशपादुका at the same time by accident which Vasiṣṭha asked Rāma to give to Bharata.

ARAṆYAKĀṆḌA

25. Sītā's story about her marriage told to Anasūyā is in the same words. अथ दीर्घस्य कालस्य राघवोयं महाद्युतिः is also found there (see Appendix 6).

26. Rāma says the same incongruous words to Śarabhaṅga.

अहमेवाहरिष्यामि स्वयं लोकान्महामुने ।
आवासं त्विहमिच्छामि प्रदिष्टमिह कानने ।।

27. We have the same tirade against slaughter from Sītā cautioning Rāma against fighting with the Rākṣasas.

28. Rāvaṇa and Mārīca discussing the possibility of Sītā's abduction, before Śūrpaṇakhā suggests it, is not to be found herein.

29. The *śloka* which suggests the interpolated nature of the story of the golden deer is partly found and partly omitted. We simply find आगमिष्यति मे भर्ता वन्यमादाय पुष्कलम् but not रुरून् गोधान् etc.

KIṢKINDHĀKĀṆḌA

30. The interpolated geographical chapters are found in the same manner, Daṇḍakāraṇya and the Godāvarī being twice mentioned, once in the south and again in the east.

31. तत्रासीनं नगस्याग्रे मलयस्य महौजसः
द्रक्ष्यथादित्यसंकाशमगस्त्यमृषिसत्तमम् ।

is also found in this text.

32. The contradiction in Sugrīva first saying "I do not know Rāvaṇa's abode" and subsequently in this geographical chapter saying "Laṅkā is that Rākṣasa's abode" is found here also. We have the same two *ślokas* in the same two places.

न जाने निलयं तस्य सर्वथा पापरक्षसः
सामर्थ्यं विक्रमं वापि दौष्कुलेयस्य वा कुलम् ।।
यत्र देवैरवध्यस्य रावणस्य दुरात्मनः ।
राक्षसाधिपतेर्वासः श्रूयते वानरर्षभाः ।।

SUNDARAKĀṆḌA

33. The *śloka* about Sītā performing *sandhyā* has been carefully omitted here. But it is difficult to conceive how Māruti expected her there. We have simply the line—इह सा राममहिषी नूनमेष्यति जानकी.

34. No mention is made in this text also of the finding of Rāmeśvara temple or of stones floating on the sea.

YUDDHAKĀṆḌA

35. Māruti brings a mountain-top from गंधमादन but the name Droṇagiri does not occur.

36. The heads of Rāvaṇa are cut off in the same way and grow again. We have the same *śloka*,

तच्छिरः पतितं भूमौ दृष्टं लोकैस्त्रिभिस्तदा ।
तथैव सदृशं चान्यद्रावणस्योत्थितं शिरः ।।

37. The following *śloka* suitably altered is found

तस्य क्रुद्धस्य नेत्रेभ्यःप्रापतन्नश्रुबिन्दवः
दीपेभ्य इव दीप्तेभ्यः सार्चिषःस्नेहबिन्दवः ।।

But a little before this we have तस्य क्रुद्धस्य ते नेत्रे रक्ते कोपाग्निना पुनः. And also when Rāvaṇa's widows are wailing

उत्क्षिप्य च भुजौ काचिद् भूमौ विपरिवर्तते
काचिदंके शिरःकृत्वा रुरोद भृशमीक्षती ॥

38. We have as in the other text, the mention of मंदोदरी once only; also Daśaratha appearing before Rāma; also Rāma asking Brahmadeva who he is and the same *stuti* by Brahmā.

39. Rāma does not say to Sīta as they are returning in the *vimāna* अत्र पूर्वं महादेवः प्रसादमकरोन्मम but on the contrary says what had actually taken place before : *viz.*—

अत्राहं शयितो देवि कुशास्तीर्णे महीतले ।
दर्शनार्थं समुद्रस्य त्रिरात्रं नररूपिणः ॥

40. In the last benediction we have the moderate praise आसीद्वर्षशतायुश्च तथा पुत्रसहस्रवान्.

41. We have the very suggestive *śloka* as in the other text, आदिकाव्यं महच्चैतत्पुरा वाल्मीकिना कृतम्.

Before finishing this, we may give the extents of the two versions as given by Mr. Abhyankar :

Kāṇḍa	Bengal Version		Bombay Version	
	Chapters	Ślokas	Chapters	Ślokas
Bāla or Ādi	80	2292	77	2250
Ayodhyā	127	4121	119	4350
Araṇya	79	2842	75	2445
Kiṣkindhā	63	2302	67	2467
Sundara	95	3300	68	2815
Yuddha	113	4936	133	6198
Uttara			111	4003
Total	557	19793	650	24528

The excess of chapters and *ślokas* in the Bombay edition over that declared in the poem itself *viz.*, 50 in the former and 528 in the latter has, we believe, compelled the commentators to declare certain chapters and *ślokas* as interpolated.

2

DIFFERENCES BETWEEN THE RĀMOPĀKHYĀNA OF THE *MAHĀBHĀRATA* AND THE *RĀMĀYAṆA*

The following differences can be marked in the story of the Rāmopākhyāna (महाभारत-वनपर्व) and that of the present *Rāmāyaṇa* showing how the latter has increased the marvellous element.

1. Sītā is said to be the daughter of Janaka but no mention is made of her being born of the earth.

विदेहराजजनकः सीता तस्यात्मजा विभो ।
यां चकार स्वयं त्वष्टा रामस्य महिषी प्रिया ॥

This does not state that she was अयोनिजा but the commentator thinks otherwise.

2. The birth of Rāvaṇa is differently given

स राजराजो लंकायां न्यवसन्नरवाहनः
राक्षसीः प्रददौ तिस्रः पितुर्वै परिचारिकाः ।
पुष्पोत्कटा च राका च मालिनी च विशांपते
पुष्पोत्कटायां जज्ञाते कुंभकर्णदशग्रीवौ ॥
मालिनी जनयामास पुत्रमेकं विभीषणम् ।
राकायां मिथुनं जज्ञे खरशूर्पणखे तथा ॥

3. Rāma is an Avatāra of Viṣṇu. But the story of the पायस is not given in the Rāmopākhyāna.

4. The रथ of Rāvaṇa is not mentioned at the time of Sītā's abduction. He flew into the sky taking Sītā by the hair—मूर्धजेषु निजग्राह ऊर्ध्वमाचक्रमे ततः.

5. The story of the building of the *setu* is behind as well as a little ahead of the *Rāmāyaṇa;* the Sea showed himself to Rāma in a dream and told him that Nala should build a *setu*. The story of Rāma's taking out an arrow in anger against the Sea is not given. The story of stones floating on water not found in the *Rāmāyaṇa*, may perhaps have been suggested by the following *śloka*—

यत्काष्ठं वा तृणं वापि शिला 'क्षेप्स्यते मयि ।
सर्वं तद्धारयिष्यामि स ते सेतुर्भविष्यति ॥

Curiously enough the proposal to cross the sea in boats is here discussed and disposed of by Rāma as follows

नावो न संति सेनाया बह्व्यस्तारयितुं क्षमा: ।
वणिजामुपघातं च कथमस्मद्विधश्चरेत् ।
विस्तीर्णं चैव सैन्यं च हन्याच्छिद्रेण वै रिपु: ॥

The *setu* is still known, says the *Mahābhārata*,

दशयोजनविस्तारमायतं दशयोजनम् ।
नलसेतुरितिख्यातो योऽद्यापि प्रथितो भुवि ॥

6. Kumbhakarṇa is killed here by Lakṣmaṇa.

7. Indrajit fought unseen and made Rāma and his brother insensible. They were brought round by Sugrīva with the aid of herbs used with supernatural incantations

विशल्यौ चापि सुग्रीव: क्षणेनेतौ चकार ह ।
विशल्यया महौषध्या दिव्यमंत्रप्रयुक्तया ॥

There is no mention of the Sañjīvanī herb being brought from the Himalayas by Māruti.

8. Rāvaṇa is said to have been simply burnt alive by *brahmāstra*. There is no mention of his heads being cut off several times and new heads rising in their place as stated in the *Rāmāyaṇa* of Vālmīki.

9. Sītā does not go through fire ordeal but there is an *ākāśavāṇī* of Vāyu and Agni testifying to her purity.

3

SOME EXCELLENT SAYINGS IN THE *RĀMĀYAṆA*

मा निषाद प्रतिष्ठां त्वमगम: शाश्वती: समा: ।
यत्क्रौंचमिथुनादेकमवधी: काममोहितम् ॥
धिग्बलं क्षत्रियबलं ब्रह्मतेजोबलं बलम् ।
सह रंस्ये त्वया वीर वनेषु मधुगंधिषु ॥
रामं दशरथं विद्धि मां विद्धि जनकात्मजाम् ।
अयोध्यामटवीं विद्धि गच्छ तात यथासुखम् ॥

यथा फलानां पक्वानां नान्यत्र पतनाद्भयम् ।
तथा नरस्य जातस्य नान्यत्र मरणाद्भयम् ॥
वयसः पतमानस्य स्रोतसो वाऽनिवर्तिनः ।
आत्मा सुखे नियोक्तव्यः सुखभाजः प्रजाः स्मृताः ॥
अन्तकाले हि भूतानि मुह्यन्तीति पराश्रुतिः ॥
सुलभाः पुरुषा राजन् सततं प्रियवादिनः ।
अप्रियस्य च पथ्यस्य वक्ता श्रोता च दुर्लभः ॥
गुणवान् वा परजनः स्वजनो निर्गुणोपि वा ।
निर्गुणः स्वजनः श्रेयान् यः परः पर एव सः ॥
यः स्वपक्षं परित्यज्य परपक्षं निषेवते ।
स स्वपक्षे क्षयं याते पश्चात्तैरेव हन्यते ॥
एति जीवन्तमानन्दो नरं वर्षशतादपि ।
श्रूयते हस्तिभिर्गीतः श्लोको पद्मवने पुरा ।
नाग्निर्नान्यानि शस्त्राणि न नः पाशा भयावहाः ।
घोराः स्वार्थप्रयुक्तास्तु ज्ञातया नो भयावहाः ॥
सागरं चांबरप्रख्यमंबरं सागरोपमम् ।
रामरावणयोर्युद्धं रामरावणयोरिव ॥
संप्राप्तमवमानं यस्तेजसा न प्रमार्जति ।
कस्तस्य पौरुषेणार्थो महताप्यल्पचेतसः ॥

4

DAŚARATHA JĀTAKA

(Extracts from translation by V. Fausboll)

"Come Lakkhaṇa and Sītā." This the master related while living at Jetavana concerning a householder whose father had died. For he, when his father was dead, abandoned all work and became a slave to grief. The master told a story.

In times past there lived in Vārāṇasī a great king Daśaratha by name. His queen, the head-wife of sixteen thousand women bore unto him two sons and one daughter. The elder son was the sage Rāma, the second the prince Lakkhaṇa, the daughter the princess Sītā. Afterwards the

queen died. When he had performed the necessary funeral ceremonies he set another in the place of queen. She became dear and pleasing to the king, and afterwards having conceived, bore a son. They named him prince Bharata. From love to the son the king said "My dear, I grant thee a boon, accept it." She accepted it but left it in abeyance at that time. When the prince was eight years old she went to the king and said "Lord, a boon was conferred by you upon my son, now grant it and give him the kingdom." The king snapping his fingers reprimanded her saying "Wretched outcaste, my two sons shine like masses of fire. Thou askest me to give the kingdom to thy son after having put them both to death." Terrified she entered the inner apartment; but on subsequent days she again and again asked the king for the kingdom. The king, however, not granting her that boon thought "Women are treacherous. This one either by writing false letters or by resorting to mean bribery will have my sons killed." So having summoned his sons told them the matter. He said, "Dears, if you live here there may be obstacles, go to a neighbouring kingdom or to the forest; come back at the time of my funeral and seize upon the paternal kingdom." After again calling the astrologers and asking them the limit of his life and hearing that another twelve years would pass he said "Dears, after the lapse of twelve years hence return." They said "Well", the princess Sītā saying "I too will go away with my brothers." These three having gone out surrounded by multitude of people and having after sending back the multitude gradually entered the Himavanta, built a hermitage in a region abounding with water and resided subsisting on fruits. Lakkhaṇa and Sītā demanding of the Sage Rāma said "You stand in our father's place, therefore, do you stay at the hermitage; we will bring fruits and nourish you." From that moment the Sage Rāma remains there. The others brought fruits and watched over him. While they were residing there the great king Daśaratha ended his days from sorrow for his sons in the ninth year. Having finished the funeral rites over him, the queen said "Raise the umbrella for my son prince Bharata." But the ministers did not allow it. Prince Bharata saying "I bring my brother the Sage Rāma from the forest" reached with a fourfold army his dwelling place and after halting the army at a short distance entered the hermitage at a time when the sage Lakkhaṇa and Sītā had gone to the forest. Having approached the Sage Rāma who was sitting at ease and without desires at the door of the hermitage like a fixed golden statue and having bowed to him he told him the tidings of the king's death and fell down at his feet. The Sage Rāma neither grieved nor wept. There was not even the slightest commotion of his senses. While Bharata was weeping the other two came back bringing various kinds of fruits. Sage Rāma thought "These are young, they have no discriminating understanding as I have; their hearts will break, I'll get them to go down into the water and then I will tell them these tidings." Then showing them a pool in front of them he said "At length you have come. This be your punishment, go down into this water and stay there." He at the same time pronounced the first half stanza.

> "Come Lakkhaṇa and Sītā both go down into the water.

They at his mere call went down and stayed. Then he pronounced the other half stanza

> "Thus says this Bharata, the king Daśaratha is dead."[1]

Hearing the tidings of their father's death they became insensible. He again told them and they again became insensible. Thus for the third time having become insensible the attendants raised them up out of the water. They all sat mutually crying and lamenting. Prince Bharata asked "By what strength, Oh Rāma, dost thou not mourn what is to be mourned." Then the Sage Rāma said "What cannot be preserved by man even if much bewailed, for such a thing's sake why should the wise man dis-

1. See footnote on next page.

tress himself. As ripe fruits always are in danger of falling so born mortals are always in danger of death[1] etc. etc." The assembly having heard this religious discourse of the Sage Rāma became free from sorrow, when prince Bharata bowing to the Sage Rāma said "Accept the kingdom of Vārāṇasī." "My dear take Lakkhaṇa and the princess Sītā and go and rule the kingdom. My father said to me, 'After the lapse of twelve years then come and rule.' If I go now I shall not fulfil his words but having passed three years more I'll come." "Who will reign during that time ? We shall not." "Well then until my return these shoes shall reign." So saying he took off his straw-shoes and gave them to Bharata. The three persons having taken the shoes went to Vārāṇasī. The ministers after placing the straw-shoes on the royal couch consider the case. If it be badly considered the shoes strike against each other. The Sage Rāma at the end of three years entered the city with a large retinue and having ascended the upper story of the magnificent palace Suchandaka, he from that time reigned with justice during 16 thousand years and went to heaven :

दशवर्षसहस्राणि षष्ठिवर्षशतानि च
कंबुग्रीवो महाबाहु रामो राज्यमकारयत् ॥[1]

The Master having given this instruction summed up the *Jātaka* thus—"At that time the great king Daśaratha was the great king Śuddhodana; the mother of Rāma Mahāmāyā, Sītā the mother of Rāhula, Bharata Ānanda Lakkhaṇa Sariputta, the assembly the assembly of Buddha and the Sage Rāma myself."

5

RĀKṢASA NAMES

The names of the Rākṣasas found in the *Rāmāyaṇa* are, it will be interesting to remark, all based on their per-

1. These *ślokas* are to be found with slight variations in the *Rāmāyaṇa* of Vālmīki.

sonal peculiarities. Rāvaṇa, to begin with, means the Roarer. His other names Daśmukha or Daśagrīva mean ten-headed or ten-necked. His brother's name Kumbhakarṇa means pot-eared. Vibhīṣaṇa means terrible. Meghanāda was the name of Rāvaṇa's son and meant having a voice like the thunder. Śūrpaṇakhā his sister was fan-nailed. Her brother was Khara or an ass and Dūṣaṇa, the blamed. Rāvaṇa's generals also had names given on the same principle. Triśira was three-headed. Dhūmrakṣa had smoke-coloured-eyes. Prahasta was long-armed. These and other names were all imaginary and were not the real names of these Rākṣasas. The only name which has an aboriginal and true ring is that of the family of Rāvaṇa *viz.*, Salaṅkatāṭaṅka which fortunately still exists in the whole *Rāmāyaṇa* as a proof, though solitary, of the fact that the Rākṣasas were a real aboriginal race of cannibals like the Aztecs.

6

WAS SĪTĀ'S MARRIAGE A CHILD-MARRIAGE ?

It is maintained by many that Sītā's marriage was a child-marriage and several *ślokas* in the *Rāmāyaṇa* of Vālmīki appear to support the idea. In the Araṇyakāṇḍa where Sītā relates her own story to Rāvaṇa she says

अष्टादश हि वर्षाणि मम जन्म निगण्यते ॥

"I was 18 years old" when Rāma was banished from Ayodhyā. She states in the same place that she had lived 12 years in the family of the Ikṣvākus; and thus her age at the time of her marriage was only six. The interpolated nature of this line will however appear clear from the following considerations. In her conversation with Atri's wife at the end of the Ayodhyākāṇḍa, Sītā says

पतिसंयोगसुलभं वयो दृष्ट्वा तु मे पिता
चिंतामभ्यगमद्दीनो वित्तनाशादिवाधन: ।
तत्र दृष्ट्वा धनु:श्रेष्ठं गौरवाद्गिरिसन्निभम्
अभिवाद्य नृपा जग्मुरशक्तास्तस्य तोलने

सुदीर्घस्य तु कालस्य राघवोयं महाद्युतिः ।
विश्वामित्रेण सहितो यज्ञं द्रष्टुं समागतः ॥

"My father seeing me grown up to an age fit for union with a husband, became greatly anxious. Princes came and saw the great bow, heavy as a mountain and not able to lift it up went back. A very long time after this came Rāma in company with Viśvāmitra to see the sacrifice." (at Janaka's house). About this incident again, Janaka, says to Viśvāmitra in the Bālakāṇḍa—"The princes who went away unsuccessful became enraged and having combined invested Mithilā. For one year I fought with them and lost all my forces. In anxiety I performed *tapa* to please the gods and they gave me divine weapons with which the princes were at last defeated." It would thus appear that Janaka proclaimed his *pāṇa* or marriage vow when Sītā became of a fit age for being united with a husband. Even if this merely means fit for being married she must at least have finished her sixth year for no girl can properly be married before that time (see षडब्दमध्ये नोद्वाह्या etc). Now the princes came to try to lift up the bow and having failed invested Janaka's town and more than one year elapsed before the investment was raised. Between these events and the appearance of Rāma a very long time elapsed according to Sītā herself. How could then she possibly be only six years old when she was married to Rāma ? But the absurdity of this idea is completely exposed by the following *śloka* in the Bālakāṇḍa :

अभिवाद्याभिवाद्यांश्च सर्वा राजसुतास्तदा
रेमिरे मुदिताः सर्वा भर्तृभिःसहिता रहः ॥

[When the married couples came to Ayodhyā from Janaka's city after marriage, the *śloka* states that the princesses having bowed to those who deserved to be saluted, being delighted sported with their husbands *in private*]. Is it not ridiculous to say that a girl of six sported with her husband in private ? It is impossible to understand the word रहः in any other sense and the conclusion forces itself upon one's mind that Sītā must at least have been fifteen years old at the time of her marriage. Rāma may have been about seventeen or eighteen or even sixteen but considering that a prince at sixteen is fit for marriage and that Rāma was of an exhuberant growth and prodigious strength capable of lifting up a heavy bow, even his age cannot be said to be early at the time of his marriage.

The fact is that when in modern times child-marriage became universal, the latest editions of the Purāṇas gave their own versions of the marriage with details as to age. One such version is noted by the commentator himself and rejected by him as absurd on other grounds, *viz.*, that of the अग्निवेश्य रामायण wherein it is stated

राम: पंचदशे वर्षे षड्वर्षामपि मैथिलीम् ।
उपयेमे त्वयोध्यायां द्वादशाद्वानुवास स: ।।

(see the commentary at the end of canto CX of the Yuddhakāṇḍa). *Ślokas* like these seem to have led to the insertion of a few lines here and there, like the one given above[1], in the all-respected work of Vālmīki, supporting the modern prevalent practice of child-marriage.

7

DID RĀMA PRECEDE KṚṢṆA ?

When did Rāma live ? That is a question which we have not attempted to solve. It is indeed a question the solution of which seems to be beyond the scope of reasonable research. There are no definite data available on the subject. No foreign writer throws any light on it nor does any Indian writing supply us with any reliable clue. The *Rāmāyaṇa* of Vālmīki has itself nothing to say on the point. Modern astrologers give a horoscope of Rāma and Bharata on the basis of an interpolated *śloka* in the *Rāmāyaṇa.* Even if the horoscope is not imaginary it is too indefinite to afford any basis for calculation. The orthodox opinion prevalent in these days is that Rāma lived in the *tretā* age not of this cycle but of three cycles behind it as

1. This line *viz.*, अष्टादश हि वर्षाणि मम जन्म निगद्यते is not found in Gorresio's text.

we learn from the commentary at the end of canto CX of Yuddhakāṇḍa. A native astrologer gives the date of Rāma's fight with Rāvaṇa as 1,25,67,101 B.C. From this fabulous figure not at all inconsistent with the hyperbolical character of the *Rāmāyaṇa*, we have to turn on the other side to the opinion of Talboys Wheeler who puts Rāma down to the 10th century A.D. Many believe however that Rāma lived some time after Kṛṣṇa and before Buddha thus assigning him a date between 1500 to 500 B.C. according to their view of Kṛṣṇa's date. The real question, therefore, is whether Rāma preceded Kṛṣṇa or followed him. There are various arguments which go to prove that he must have preceded Kṛṣṇa by several centuries. If thirty nine kings intervened between him and Kṛṣṇa, as Mr. Abhyankar states on the authority of the *Viṣṇupurāṇa* and if we assign to the *Mahābhārata* the orthodox date *viz.* 3101 B.C., we may believe that Rāma lived about 3881 B.C. or taking 1500 as the date of Kṛṣṇa (arrived at by Mr. Tilak and others on the evidence of the self-same *Viṣṇupurāṇa*) and an interval of 780 years between Rāma and Kṛṣṇa we may put him in 2280 B.C. We proceed to state the arguments which lead us to think that Rāma preceded Kṛṣṇa noticing the arguments to the contrary incidentally.

The first and the foremost argument appears to be that Daṇḍakāraṇya extended in Rāma's time as far north as the Yamunā. Had it not been so Rāma could not have first taken up his abode on the Citrakūṭa hill which lies a little to the south of the Yamunā. In fact there were only a few Brahmin settlements even between the Ganges and the Yamunā such as those of Bharadvāja and Vālmīki. The state of the country in Rāma's time appears from the *Rāmāyaṇa* to have been as follows : The Aryans had taken hold of the Punjab and the country to the north of the Ganges as far east as Bihar. Settlements were being effected in the Doab while bolder adventures were pushing still further south as far as the Godāvarī; but they were exposed to the inroads of the terrible Rākṣasas or cannibals. There were no Aryan kingdoms in the Doab and none at all to the south of the Yamunā. In Kṛṣṇa's time the Aryans had settled in the valley of the Yamunā on either sides, in Central India, in Gujarat and even in the Deccan. There were clearly Aryan kingdoms in Kathiawar, Gujarat, Malwa, and Berars in Kṛṣṇa's time. Against this strong argument, it is sometimes argued that a civil war in the north must precede the colonisation of the South. We do not know why it should be so believed. On the contrary, the opposite statement would be more correct. Had there been room for fresh settlement in new and fertile lands, it seems unlikely that Yudhiṣṭhira would have fought that terrible war with the Kurus. Had the Boers any space available where they could have moved out and set up an independent kingdom, they would certainly have availed themselves of it as they did in the past and would not have fought an unequal fight with great Britain. Colonisation again does not afford any index as to sequence in time. Some portions of the Central Provinces are being brought under cultivation for the first time in these days under British rule though the country to the south of that province had been appropriated by man ages before.

Secondly, the state of the society equally with the state of the country goes to prove that Rāma must have lived in an earlier age than Kṛṣṇa and the Pāṇḍavas. Brahmins and Kṣatriyas were equally versed in the Vedas as well as in archery in Rama's days. Rāma himself could recite Vedic *mantras* and perform Vedic sacrifices like any Brahmin versed in the Vedas *e.g.* ब्रह्मवत्क्षत्रवच्चैव जजाप हित-मात्मन: and again देवता देवसंकाश यजस्व कुशलोह्यसि. In the days of the Pāṇḍavas, the two castes had so far differentiated that proficiency in the Vedas was looked down upon among the Kṣatriyas as not a very worthy qualification. Brahmin warriors were also being depreciated as Droṇa is frequently called a ब्रह्मबंधु or a depraved Brahmin for his warrior calling. The position of women was also superior in Rāma's time. They[1] could perform *sandhyā* as also

1. Probably Rāma's time was that time when
पुराकल्पे तु नारीणां मौंजीबंधनमिष्यते

sacrifice as Sītā and Kausalyā are represented doing. No woman in the *Mahābhārata*, not even the Brahmavādini Draupadī is described as performing any of these Vedic duties. It must be stated here that the *Mahābhārata* as it exists today is no doubt more ancient than the *Rāmāyaṇa* as it is today. But we are here basing our observations on such sentiments in both as are obviously archaic and as have been preserved in them through a feeling of veneration attached to old ideas.

It is sometimes argued from the raid of cattle which Duryodhana made in the country of the Virāṭas that in the days of the Pāṇḍavas, the Aryans were not an agricultural but a pastoral people while in Rāma's time they were undoubtedly agricultural. Kṛṣṇa himself, it is added, belonged to a tribe which depended more on cattle breeding than on agriculture. This is however a mistaken idea or rather inference. The Aryans of India were at no time a pastoral people. In fact the very name which they had assumed and in which they exulted *viz. ārya* indicated that they were cultivators. The keeping and rearing of large herds of the bovine cattle will be easily explained when we remember that the ancient Aryans were a beaf-eating race. Herds of cattle were thus a precious possession and a prize in war. The last Boer war shows how herds of cattle were often seized with eagerness by both parties as prizes and were even objects of a raid. The Mahomedan rulers of India always maintained large herds of cows and oxen as a department of the state. Even in the *Rāmāyaṇa*, Rāma is represented as having a large number of cows which he gave away to a Brahmin on the eve of his departure for the Daṇḍaka forest. Moreover, if Kṛṣṇa lived the life of a cattle-grazer, Rāma lived the still more primitive life of a hunter; for he is represented to have subsisted solely and for fourteen years on the flesh of deer and other beasts of the jungle.

Thirdly, long established tradition in India has it that Rāma is one of the ancient kings of India. He is mentioned among the sixteen great Kings of antiquity who are enumerated in the Ṣoḍaśa-rājīya-ākhyāna of the *Mahābhārata*. This *ākhyāna* is very old as we have already shown in our first volume. It gives a description of several kings in nearly the same words as the *Śatapatha Brāhmaṇa*. Rāma is again mentioned in the *Mahābhārata* among the kings who are described by Nārada as seated in the *sabhā* of Yama. Here be it remembered, he is not represented as an Avatāra of Viṣṇu but only as a mortal who has attained that exalted position by his great merits. He is clearly thus a predecessor of the Pāṇḍavas.

रामो दाशरथिश्चैव लक्ष्मणोथ प्रतर्दनः ।
तथापरे सहस्राणि ये गताः शशबिन्दवः ॥
इष्ट्वाश्वमेधैर्बहुभिर्महद्भिर्भूरिदक्षिणैः ॥
तस्यां सभायां राजेंद्र वैवस्वतमुपासते ॥ सभा० अ० ८

It may perhaps be thought that this mention of Rāma in the Ṣoḍaśa-rājīya-ākhyāna finds no support in the *Śatapatha Brāhmaṇa* where the great Aśvamedha sacrificers of antiquity are mentioned. As we have pointed out in our first volume, this kind of negative argument is always deceptive. The *Śatapatha Brāhmaṇa* (*kāṇḍa* 13) does not profess to give an exhaustive list of all the ancient horse-sacrificers. Not only would it be outside the scope of the *Śatapatha Brāhmaṇa* but it would even be impossible to give such a list. Yudhiṣṭhira has not been mentioned in that list and yet we would not be justified in holding that he lived after the *Śatapatha Brāhmaṇa* was composed or that Rāma for the self-same reason is posterior to it. In fact Mr. Tilak who uses this argument in the case of Yudhiṣṭhira believes that Rāma belongs to the Vedic period inasmuch as his name is to be found in a certain verse of the *Ṛgveda*. And yet Rāma is not mentioned among the horse-sacrificers of antiquity by the *Śatapatha Brāhmaṇa*. The real explanation is that it does not intend to give an exhaustive list.

From all these arguments we are inclined to think that Rāma was an ancient king of India who preceded Kṛṣṇa by several centuries. Some may be disposed to ask how was it possible for a king who ruled in Ayodhyā at a time when the whole of India to the south of the Yamunā was either an uninhabited forest or in possession of strange races to have plunged so far in the south as to conquer the island of Laṅkā. But this need not strike us as strange. Allauddin Khilji made a raid as far south as Daulatabad when the Mahomedan rule did not extend beyond the Yamunā. And when he came to the throne his general Malik Kafur plundered the country as far south as the southern ocean. Nor need it be thought that Rāma's adventure is imaginary because he was almost alone. Many a modern adventurers in India and elsewhere have gone singly among strange peoples and acquired renown and glory. If Stanley made a journey in the heart of Africa covered by jungles untouched since creation by foreign peoples, it need not be wondered that Rāma invaded and conquered Laṅkā by the assistance of native tribes in far by-gone times.